Jakob Nielsen
Raluca Budiu

Mobile
Usability

VOICES
THAT
MATTER™

New
Riders

Mobile Usability

Jakob Nielsen and Raluca Budiu

New Riders
1249 Eighth Street
Berkeley, CA 94710

Find us on the Web at www.newriders.com
To report errors, please send a note to errata@peachpit.com

New Riders is an imprint of Peachpit, a division of Pearson Education.

Senior Editor: Susan Rimerman
Copy Editor: Anne Marie Walker
Proofer: Emily K. Wolman
Indexer: James Minkin
Production Editor: Tracey Croom
Composition: Danielle Foster
Cover Design: Peachpit Press

ISBN-13: 978-0-321-88448-0
ISBN-10: 0-321-88448-5

9 8 7 6 5 4 3 2 1

Printed and bound in the United States of America

For Hannah.

　—Jakob

For Matei and Mihai, with love.

　—Raluca

Acknowledgments

We have drawn from several Nielsen Norman Group projects in writing this book. Janelle Estes ran studies of how users read from mobile devices, and Marieke McCloskey ran studies on how people read from tablets and e-readers, and also helped with some of the logistics for our Dutch study. Hoa Loranger, Kara McCain, Amy Schade, and Kathryn Whitenton helped with several of our usability studies, and Kara McCain also redesigned several screens that are shown in this book as examples of improved usability. Luice Hwang set up facilities for a large number of studies in other states and countries. Susan Pernice managed participant recruiting for studies in Australia and Netherlands. And the rest of the Nielsen Norman Group, including Jen Cardello, Susan Farrell, Garrett Godlfield, Don Norman, Kara Pernice, and Bruce Tognazzini, shared with us their personal stories and insights about mobile apps and websites.

The visioneering concepts shown in Chapter 6 were created by a team that included Bruce Tognazzini, Amy Gallaher, and Shuli Gilutz. Marc Ramsay ran our WAP phones studies in 2000. Scott Butler and the Ovo Studios generously provided us with a mobile device camera that we used for some of our studies. Hannah Kain, Aaron Katske, and Brandon Marugg helped with facilities for many of our research studies in California. Cristian Lupsa and the magazine *Decât o revistă* let us use their location and amenities during our study in Romania, and Eric Chow recruited participants for our Hong Kong study. Mihai Budiu lent us his phone for our Windows Phone 7 studies, kindly offered technical support and advice, and contributed additional insights. And finally, a special thanks to our editors Susan Rimerman, Anne Marie Walker, and Tracey Croom for all their hard work with the manuscript.

About the Authors

Jakob Nielsen

Jakob Nielsen, Ph.D., is a principal of Nielsen Norman Group. He is the founder of the "discount usability engineering" movement, which emphasizes fast and efficient methods for improving the quality of user interfaces. Nielsen, noted as "the world's leading expert on Web usability" by *U.S. News and World Report* and "the next best thing to a true time machine" by *USA Today*, is the author of the best-selling book *Designing Web Usability: The Practice of Simplicity* (New Riders Publishing, 2000), which has sold more than a quarter of a million copies in 22 languages.

His other books include *Usability Engineering* (Morgan Kaufmann, 1993); with Robert L. Mack, *Usability Inspection Methods* (Wiley, 1994); *Multimedia and Hypertext: The Internet and Beyond* (Morgan Kaufmann, 1995); *International User Interfaces* (Wiley, 1996); with Marie Tahir, *Homepage Usability: 50 Websites Deconstructed* (New Riders Publishing, 2001); with Hoa Loranger, *Prioritizing Web Usability* (New Riders Publishing, 2006); and with Kara Pernice, *Eyetracking Web Usability* (New Riders Publishing, 2010). Nielsen's Alertbox column on Web usability at www.useit.com has been published on the Internet since 1995 and has approximately 200,000 readers.

From 1994 to 1998, Nielsen was a Sun Microsystems Distinguished Engineer. His previous affiliations include Bell Communications Research, the Technical University of Denmark, and the IBM User Interface Institute. He has been awarded 80 United States patents, mainly on ways of making the Internet easier to use. Nielsen holds a Ph.D. in human-computer interaction from the Technical University of Denmark.

Raluca Budiu

Raluca Budiu, Ph.D., is a user-experience specialist with Nielsen Norman Group. There she conducts usability research; consults with large companies from a variety of industries; and presents tutorials on mobile usability, usability of touch devices, cognitive psychology for designers, and principles of human-computer interaction. She co-authored research reports on mobile usability, iPad usability, and the usability of websites for children.

From 2004 to 2007, Budiu worked at Xerox PARC doing research in human-computer interaction. She also explored new ways of measuring information scent, and conducted research on interfaces for social bookmarking systems and on the cognitive benefits of tagging. Budiu was also a user researcher at Microsoft Corporation, where she explored future directions and made strategic recommendations for incorporating user-generated content and social-Web features into MSN.

Before PARC, Budiu carried out research in psycholinguistics and cognitive science, building computational models of how people understand language.

Budiu has authored more than 20 articles and conference presentations on human-computer interaction, psychology, and cognitive science. She holds a Ph.D. from Carnegie Mellon University.

Contents

Preface

The topic of this book is simple: how to design the best websites and apps for mobile devices and tablets. How is it different from the many other books on this topic? It is based on empirical evidence on how regular users actually use such user interfaces.

A key lesson from the past decades of usability is that you cannot trust your own instincts regarding what will be easy for normal people. The fact that you're reading this book proves that you are very different from the average mobile user. Repeat after us: *"I am not the target audience"* (unless you're designing an app for designers).

Most other books on mobile design describe the authors' personal preferences: what they think is good. This can certainly be interesting information, but it's safer to rely on actual usability research with more representative users.

Chapter 1 describes how we conducted this research. You can skip it if you simply want to know what we discovered but not how we ran the studies. However, the chapter is short, so we recommend that you read it anyway. Who knows, maybe you will be inspired to conduct your own user testing when you see how easy it is to get real data.

Chapter 2 is about the question that should be addressed before doing any mobile design: Should you even have a mobile site or app?

Chapters 3 and 4 are the meat of the book: how to design for mobile devices and how to develop content for the small screen. Chapter 5 applies these concepts further to the larger tablet screens.

Chapter 6 presents a broader perspective beyond the current flat touch screens, and the appendix takes a look back at the pre-iPhone phones.

Why Mobile Is Different

In 2012 the analytics company Monetate released a study of 100 million site visits across its e-commerce clients. Conversion rates differed dramatically, depending on which device was used to access a site, as shown in the following table:

Device	Conversion Rate
Desktop computer	3.5%
Mobile phone	1.4%
Tablet	3.2%

The definition of "conversion rate" is simple. It's the percentage of visiting users who end up taking a desired action. On e-commerce sites—such as those analyzed in the table—it's even easier to understand conversion, because the "desired action" is to buy something. Thus a conversion rate of 3 percent means that of every 100 people who arrive at the site, 3 turn into paying customers and 97 leave without buying anything.

It's clear that mobile users bought much less than people sitting at their PC. It's also interesting that the conversion rates of the tablet users were much closer to the desktop users than to the phone users. As you'll see in Chapter 5, this matches our usability findings, because we have also seen that browsing websites on tablets (like the iPad) is much easier than it is to use websites on mobile phones.

What should we make of the huge difference in conversion rates between desktop computers and mobile phones? There are at least two different possible conclusions:

- The mobile user experience must be horrible. (This is in fact what we find in user testing.) Therefore there are fortunes to be made if companies would only design mobile-optimized sites that are easier to use for mobile users. After all, mobile sales could be 2.5 times greater if mobile sites were as easy to use as desktop sites.

- It's not worth investing in mobile design, because mobile users don't account for very much business. Mobile phones are fine for frivolous tasks like checking sports scores and posting Facebook updates but not for higher-value tasks.

Both conclusions are reasonable. As we discuss in Chapter 2, some companies shouldn't bother designing for mobile. But many companies should improve their mobile design to better match mobile usability guidelines, even if they don't currently get a lot of business from mobile users. It's quite likely that the small amount of business is caused by a low conversion rate, which again is caused by a design that doesn't match the special mobile needs.

So what are those special mobile usability issues? To some extent, many are not that different from the regular usability issues we have discussed in our many previous books about Web usability. The main difference is that each guideline is *even more crucial* for mobile.

For example, when we discuss writing for the Web, we've always said to be brief and to get straight to the point at the top of the page. Many users will never see the bottom of a Web page if the top of the page doesn't immediately communicate its relevance for the user's current problem. This guideline is equally true for desktop design and for mobile design. But it's stricter for mobile. On the small screen, text shouldn't just be short—it should be ultra-short. And the "top of the page" means a much smaller area on mobile.

There are two ways to consider whether mobile and desktop user experience issues are different. First, we can *empirically* say for certain that there is a measurable difference between the two classes of devices, as shown by the conversion data in the preceding table and by the user testing data we present in this book.

Second, it just makes good *common sense* to design differently for highly different devices. In the early days of the Web, we had to explain why designing Web pages was not the same as designing printed magazines or brochures. By now most people have probably come to realize that print and online are distinct media forms and require separate design approaches. Similarly, there are many differences between mobile and desktop use, such as small versus big screen, on the move versus stationary, touch versus mouse, wireless (and sometimes spotty) connectivity versus faster wired Internet, and so on.

Screen Shots Are Examples Only

We can tell you right now what the customer reviews in various online bookstores will say about this book two years from now. Many reviewers will complain that the screen shots are very old. Others will say that it's not fair to criticize companies for the way their mobile sites looked before they were redesigned (as most will hopefully be by then).

In fact, even if you bought this book the day it was published, you might feel the same: It's not fair to criticize a design that has been improved while the book was being edited and printed. The mobile field moves fast enough that many of the sites and apps shown here will surely be out in new releases by the time you lay your eager hands on a freshly printed book.

But let's make one thing clear: We don't show a screen shot to criticize the owners or designers of that site. This is not a consumer review of best mobile sites or advice for what apps to install on your phone to have a good time. We don't even care whether a specific site is good or bad, because we have no vested interest either way. We're always happy to see sites improve, because that shows uptake of our usability findings, but if a design stays the same—or gets worse—it's no skin off our nose.

We include screen shots in this book to serve as examples of our usability findings. If we expended our entire page count on elaborate discussions of abstract principles, we would have no readers. Snooze.

It's a well known, human-factors principle from instructional design that specifics communicate better than abstractions. We're simply following our own guidelines when we try to *show* you what we mean instead of purely *telling* you.

A given screen shot remains just as good of an example of a usability principle even if the company behind that site came to its senses and improved the design after we grabbed the image.

As a meta-example (an example of an example), let's say that we included a picture of Apple Computer's rainbow-striped logo from 1976 as an example of how you might employ many different colors in a logo. Well, Apple changed to a monochrome logo in 1998, but that doesn't mean that all pictures of its 1976 should be removed from discussions of how color works in logos.

In fact, sometimes older examples are better examples than newer ones if they more clearly show the underlying principle. Some usability mistakes, fortunately, are becoming so rare that they're found mainly on obscure sites that make many other design errors in the same screen, making for more confused examples. But we still must warn against usability problems that have become rare because there's always somebody who's ready to introduce a bad design that revives the mistake.

Case in point: We had *almost* eradicated splash screens from the Web after a decade-long campaign against this user-hostile design idea. No big corporation or best-selling e-commerce site will put a Flash intro in front of its homepage these days. But we've tested several mobile apps that reintroduced this user experience sin. Sure enough, our test users complained just as bitterly about these new designs as the last generation of users did about Flash intros back in 2000.

To misquote a famous saying, the price of good user experience is eternal vigilance. Old mistakes will come back to bite you (and your customers) if you don't know about them.

If you designed any of the screen shots we use in this book, rest assured that we don't mean you any harm. We're not complaining about you. We know that commercial design projects are nothing but one compromise after the next, and that design decisions are often made by old-school managers who don't understand interaction design.

The examples have no deeper meaning other than this: They make our usability findings concrete so that you can see some specific user interface designs that average people will have an easy or a difficult time using.

—*Jakob Nielsen and Raluca Budiu*

1 Our Research: How We Ran the Usability Studies

This book is different from almost all other books about mobile user interface design in one way: Our findings and recommendations are based on empirical research. We don't rely on our own opinions. We don't ask you to design the type of mobile sites and apps that we personally like and would prefer to use.

Instead, we report how a broad spectrum of average users around the world actually uses websites and apps. What do people like and dislike? What designs are easy for them to use, and what causes them trouble? We know, because we've seen it happen.

You, dear reader, are probably not an average user. Chances are that you are particularly interested in mobile devices and in user interface design. Otherwise, why did you buy this book when you could have purchased several perfectly good crime novels instead for the same price?

We (Jakob and Raluca) both have doctorates and decades of experience in the high-tech business and with user-experience research. We even live in Silicon Valley. What we personally like is completely irrelevant because we are so different from the majority of users around the globe. Don't design for us. But equally as much, don't design for yourself.

Design for your customers.

We strongly recommend that you run your own usability studies with your own customers as they attempt to use your design. You always learn something valuable every time you do this. In this chapter you'll learn more about the proper methodology for studying mobile usability.

But why not start out benefiting from the studies we've already run? The findings in this book are distilled from hundreds of hours spent observing real user behavior across many different research studies. This chapter summarizes these studies. You can skip the rest of Chapter 1 and go directly to the findings in Chapter 2 if you don't care how we know what we know.

Client Research

We conduct two types of user research: client studies and studies funded by our own company, Nielsen Norman Group. The first law of consulting is that all client information must remain confidential. Therefore, we can't tell you anything about our consulting clients or the findings from the work we've done for them. This is why we supplement our client work with a large amount of independent research. Because we pay for these studies ourselves, we're free to tell you everything that happened. The information in this book is based on this self-funded research.

Even though we can't report on the work our clients paid for, we obviously know everything that happened in those studies. Therefore, the secret client findings inform the publicly disclosed guidelines. If something previously unknown happens in a client study, we know to invest in a public study to find out more about that type of user behavior. And if a new client study confirms the findings from a public study done the year before, we know that those old findings continue to hold and we don't bother investing more in researching that issue again.

Diary Studies

Early in our mobile project, we conducted two separate diary studies to understand the range of activities that people perform on their phones. The first study involved 14 people from six different countries (Australia, Netherlands, Romania, Singapore, UK, and USA) who owned different types of phones—feature phones and smartphones, including touch-screen phones. For the second diary study, we collected data from 13 iPhone owners in the United States.

For the first diary study, we were less interested in specific usability problems; therefore, we recruited participants with relatively advanced technical skills and did not impose any of the typical occupational restrictions that are used when recruiting for traditional usability testing (for example, no IT-related occupations). For the second study, we recruited more average users who did not work in marketing or any IT-related fields.

The snippet technique was introduced by J. Brandt, N. Weiss, and S. Klemmer in txt 4 l8r: Lowering the burden for diary studies under mobile conditions (CHI, 2007).

Both diary studies used a variant of the snippet technique to make mobile logging as quick and nonintrusive as possible. Using Twitter, participants recorded every activity that they did on their mobile phone (except for talking or text messaging) for one to two weeks. Each time they used their mobile device, users tweeted a short message intended to remind them of the activity. At the end of the day, users went back to their tweets and elaborated on each of them by filling in a questionnaire that detailed the context of the corresponding mobile activity.

At the end of their participation in the diary study, we conducted a short phone interview with our users. In the second study, instead of the phone interview, participants came to the lab for a regular usability-testing session.

Twitter is a micro-blogging service that allows each user to post short messages; the messages are further broadcasted to all other Twitter users who opted to receive updates from that particular user (that is, to "follow" that user).

Usability Testing

Over the years, we carried out many mobile usability studies in the United States, but also in other countries (Australia, Hong Kong, Netherlands, Romania, and UK). All of these were traditional usability studies using the think-aloud methodology. Studies were conducted as one-on-one sessions with one test user at a time. (These were not focus groups.)

The purpose of these studies was to understand the typical usability issues that people encounter when using apps or the Web on a variety of mobile phones—including feature phones and smartphones with and without touch screens.

For most of our usability-testing sessions, users brought their own phone or tablet to our lab for individual sessions that lasted between 60 and 90 minutes. (Exception: A few of the participants in our tablet studies used a tablet that we provided.) Each session involved the participant, a facilitator, and in some cases, one or two observers. The participants started by telling us how they normally used their device and showing us some of the apps that they had installed on their device. Next, we gave each participant tasks to complete; these tasks involved either the Web or mobile apps. Users commented on:

- What they were looking for or reading

- What they liked or did not like about the site

- What made it easy or difficult for them to accomplish the task

Some of the tasks were directed to specific websites or apps (for example, Use espn.go.com to find out if there are any NBA basketball games that you could watch tonight on the ESPN TV channel); others were open-ended (such as, Find where the word "dollar" comes from), requiring users to first choose one or more appropriate websites or apps before solving the problem with those sites or apps. For the directed tasks, users had to find and install the app on their phone, or in the case of websites, had to find a way to get to the site on their phone.

Table 1.1 provides examples of the tasks that users performed. The open-ended tasks let users decide what app or website they would use to complete the task. The directed tasks indicate the app or website that the users had to use.

Overall, 124 users participated in our phone usability testing sessions and another 35 users in our tablet sessions for a total of 159 users. All of them used their phone several times per week for activities other than texting or talking. We screened out for technical experts and people who worked in usability or marketing, because they were not the target users for the sites we tested and tend to exhibit atypical behaviors due to their expertise.

In most of our studies, the participants' interaction with the phone was recorded using a document camera. For a few studies we used a mobile device camera mounted on the phone. The document camera and the mobile device camera allowed the participants to hold the phone in their hands.

Mobile Usability

Table 1.1 Examples of Tasks Used in Our Usability Testing

Open-ended Tasks	Directed Tasks
Find the symptoms of swine flu and what you should do to avoid getting sick.	Use yelp.com to find reviews of the San Francisco restaurant Absinthe.
Check the local weather forecast for tonight.	You have $50 to spend on a piece of clothing for yourself. Use the JC Penney app to find something that you might like.
You want to get some dessert and a drink late after a movie. Find a place that serves good desserts and that is open after 10 p.m.	You want to buy some pasta, diced tomatoes, and ice cream. Use the Coles app to create a list that contains all those items.
Your friend wants to watch a movie on TV tonight after 8 p.m. Find a listing of tonight's TV program and identify a movie that she may want to watch.	Using the app AA Stocks, find the current stock value of China Mobile. How did the stock change during the past month?
Find a *Tom and Jerry* video cartoon.	Use the app Flipboard for the iPad to check the latest news. Set up the app to show the news topics that interest you.
It's 6 p.m. and you need to get from West Kensington to Tufnell Park. You decide to take the underground. Find out the best way to get there, changing as few lines as possible.	You want to take a photograph of the Golden Gate Bridge from the vista point. Use the app LightTrac to find the direction of the sun's rays tomorrow at noon.

Qualitative User Research

If you're an old-school marketing person, you probably won't find it very impressive that we tested 159 users in our mobile usability studies. (We tested additional users in our original research on WAP [Wireless Application Protocol] phones and in various other studies of primitive pre–iPhone mobile designs that we mainly won't discuss here.)

We're not trying to predict whether iPhone or Android will sell more units among the "Millennial" demographic next quarter. Equally, we're not trying to measure unaided recall of a particular brand name or even customer attitudes toward a brand.

We study behavior, not opinions. We study specific user interface designs and if users have a difficult time or an easy time accomplishing tasks with each design option. This type of research is best done in a qualitative manner, not by collecting statistics from large numbers of users.

As an analogy, consider the design of carpeting for a hospital corridor. If you observe a few elderly patients with walkers who trip over a bump in the carpet, you could reasonably conclude that *carpet bumps cause a usability problem for elderly patients* and recommend that the hospital installs smooth carpeting.

In 1999, Jakob Nielsen wrote the first book about website usability: *Designing Web Usability: The Practice of Experience* (Peachpit Press). Because the cover was strikingly blue and green, many people remember this as the "blue-green book."

Designing Web Usability was based on about the same amount of usability testing as we have conducted for the present book: fewer than 200 users. This was more than enough to identify all the big issues in Web usability—people's reluctance to wait for slow downloads, their distaste for splash screens, their quick and somewhat superficial scanning of most of the content, and so forth.

Initially, some proponents of cool design were skeptical of the message in *Designing Web Usability*. But today it's safe to say that any company that tries to actually conduct business on the Internet has bought into most of the recommendations from this early book.

Even though one data point can't prove anything conclusively, it is reasonable to expect *Mobile Usability* (this book) to have the same fate as *Designing Web Usability* (the 1999 book). Initially, some designers may be hostile to findings that contradict their personal preferences, but in a few years the usability research will be accepted as common wisdom. By reading the book now, you have the option of being ahead of this curve and can start acting on the recommendations before everybody else does so, as a matter of course.

(*Designing Web Usability* was a great book for its time—if we do say so ourselves. But it was written in 1999, when the Internet was a more primitive beast. If you want to know the current recommendations on Web usability, we now prefer that you read our newer books *Prioritizing Web Usability* [Peachpit Press, 2006] and *Eyetracking Web Usability* [Peachpit Press, 2009], which are based on research with several thousand test users.)

You don't need to observe 1000 old folks meandering down the hallways and count how many of them trip. You also shouldn't wait until the hospital is sued because a poor old lady fell and broke her hip.

Statistics showing that, say, 13.2 percent of patients trip over the bump might look impressive on a slide show to convince management to invest in better carpets. And the malpractice suit would certainly concentrate the executive mind-set. But the recommendation to install safer carpeting could be made after an afternoon's observational research.

Once you've seen a problem in real life, you know it's there. You don't need to measure it.

In addition, we can estimate the magnitude of a problem with a much smaller number of users than what's needed to measure it precisely. Does it really matter whether 63 or 65 percent of users have difficulty with a certain design element? If a simpler study finds that "most" users have difficulty, that's enough to avoid that design.

As another example, let's say that a website is about to publish an article about the H5N1 influenza using the headline "Burd Flu Outbreak in Hong Kong." The copy editor will hopefully flag "Burd" as a typo and suggest "Bird" as the correct spelling. Even if you had only one person review the draft copy, that's enough to identify the error and the fix. You don't need to poll 1000 editors to see how many of them agree that "bird" is spelled with an "i" instead of a "u."

Admittedly, some usability problems are so subtle that it's not enough to see them once. But observing 159 people across four continents is more than enough to understand any big issues. In this book we have only enough page count to discuss issues that are so important that our amount of qualitative research is more than sufficient to nail down what constitutes good or bad design.

We are not researching minor design issues that might make a one percent difference to the business value of a mobile site or app. We hunt big game, so we pack our elephant gun.

Obviously, for large companies, one percent can mean hundreds of thousands of dollars, so they should invest in more detailed research to resolve the small usability issues in their design. However, even the largest company is well advised to start its mobile usability research with smaller, qualitative studies, which will no doubt quickly find several major usability problems that should be addressed before moving on to any fine-tuning of the user interface.

Two final points for anybody who still questions qualitative user research:

- Empirical evidence from countless projects over the last 23 years shows that testing with a handful of users is sufficient to identify the majority of important usability problems in a design. Not everything will be represented, but the big findings will be there. For the purposes of this book, we don't need to know every last usability issue for any of the individual sites and apps we tested. It's more important to learn the big picture from comparing the main findings across designs to identify the general usability guidelines that everybody should know.

- Ask yourself how our 159 study participants compare with the number of actual customers you have personally observed performing test tasks in one-on-one settings. In most companies, our number will be bigger than your number. Thus, the lessons from our research will magnify the amount of empirical insights available to most design teams.

2 Mobile Strategy

Running our first mobile usability studies with modern phones in 2009 was a cringe-worthy experience for users and researchers. In terms of the user experience (UX) quality we observed, it was like stepping into a time machine for a quick trip back to 1998. The similarities between the mobile user experience in 2009 and regular desktop use of the Web in 1998 were numerous:

- **Abysmal success rates** were the norm. Users failed more often than they succeeded when using their mobiles to perform tasks on websites.

- **Download times** dominated the user experience. Most pages took far too long to load, particularly on non-3G phones. But even the highest-end phones delivered much slower browsing than a desktop computer. As a result, users were reluctant to request additional pages and they gave up easily.

- **Scrolling** caused major usability problems, especially because users often had to struggle with sites that were not optimized for mobile. In contrast to the 1990s, the problem was not that users didn't scroll, it's that they scrolled too much. On mobiles they had to move their minuscule peephole back and forth so often that they lost track of where they were and what was on the page. Often they scrolled right past something without noticing it.

In **Figure 2.1**(A-C) we show the different stages through which the full site of NBC.com went as it slowly loaded on a mobile device at full connectivity on the AT&T network. When the page was finally loaded, it was difficult to make sense of the many images and links on the site without zooming in. Zooming into the page allowed users to read more easily, but they lost context: It was harder to know where they were on the page and what else was available.

The effect of the reduced viewable area on users was strongly reminiscent of usability issues we found in tests with low-vision users (Figure 2.1D). Using a mobile phone makes you a disabled user, and we all know that most sites ignore accessibility.

- **Bloated pages** made users lose context and feel lost. Most of the sites we studied wouldn't seem bloated on today's upsized PC monitors, but when rendered on a mobile, they fairly explode with bloat. Users were frequently stumped by big images or by long pages that buried the items they wanted to see.

- **Unfamiliarity** with a browser's user interface (UI) limited users' options. People used their devices suboptimally because they didn't understand the UI.

- **JavaScript crashes** and problems with advanced media types, such as video, caused more difficulties.

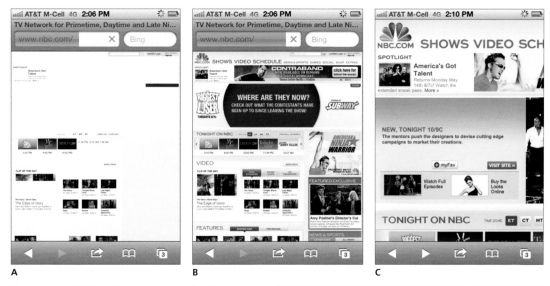

A　　　　　　　　　　B　　　　　　　　　　C

Figure 2.1 (**A**)–(**B**) The different stages through which the full site of NBC.com went as it loaded on a mobile phone. (**C**) Zooming into the page made the content readable but obscured the global context for that content. (**D**) A desktop screen shot of NBC.com when accessed in the browser with a screen magnifier.

D

Figure 2.2 Fandango's Android app allows users to pay by credit card or by using PayPal. We found that some users are more likely to make a purchase using PayPal.

Figure 2.3 PayPal's Android app supports mobile use by allowing users to authenticate via an easier-to-type four-digit PIN instead of a password.

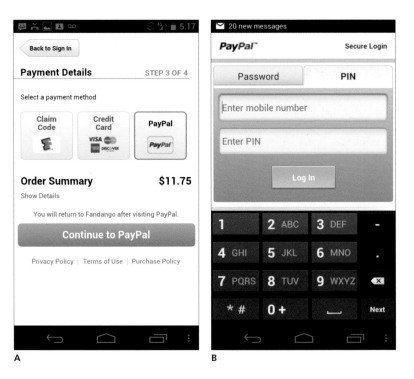

A

B

Some users are more likely to make a purchase using PayPal for two reasons: 1) They don't have to enter long credit card numbers; and 2) they think their transaction is more secure because they are not sharing the credit card information with the site.

- **Reluctance** to use websites on the mobile for many tasks was obvious, and was especially true for shopping or other tasks that required using credit cards or spending money (**Figure 2.2** and **Figure 2.3**).
- **Search dominated** Web behavior. People turned to search engines at the slightest provocation. Indeed, the users' search engine is usually the first place they go when given a new task.
- **Old-media design** was used as a model for mobile. In the 1990s, many site designs mimicked good-looking print publications and offered weak interaction support. In 2009, sites were designed as, well, websites. More specifically, they were designed as desktop websites, and that's the wrong media form for mobile use; even on the best phones, driving the interaction is painful, and simple designs are a must.

  Self-looping carousels are one example of a feature copied from the desktop that doesn't work well on mobile (**Figure 2.4**). Because the screen is small, users will often scroll down quickly, pushing the carousel above the fold and out of view. The automated looping through the different carousel items is thus wasted, because the user can no longer see the carousel.

Top navigation bars (**Figure 2.5**), although popular on the desktop, also don't always translate well on mobile. Issues occur, especially when they contain too many items: The designer is either forced to make them too small (and thus harder to touch reliably)—as in Figure 2.5A—or needs to expand the navigation bar so it takes too much space onscreen—as in Figure 2.5B.

Figure 2.4 IGN (m.ign.com). The carousel at the top of the screen is automatically moving to the next story and often gets ignored by users.

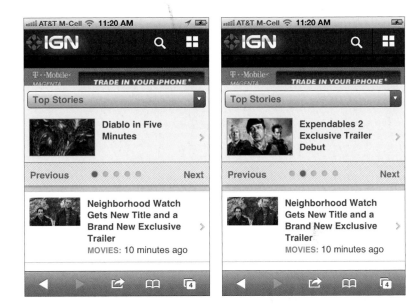

Figure 2.5 Top navigation bars on two different sites: (**A**) *Sports Illustrated* (m.si.com) and (**B**) *Entertainment Weekly* (m.ew.com).

A

B

Year after year, our newer studies continue to confirm most of these basic impressions from the first study. Today, user experience on mobile is certainly getting better, because more and more sites have built mobile-optimized versions, and designers now have a better understanding of what works on the small screen. However there's still a lot of interaction pain in doing tasks on mobile phones. So what changed since 2009? Here's what changed:

- The overall task success rates are slowly getting better, especially when users turn to apps.

- Users are more familiar with their phones. Since 2009 the mobile landscape has changed significantly. According to a survey done by the Nielsen Company in May 2012, over half of Americans own a smartphone, and only two platforms dominate the smartphone market: the iPhone and the Android. Although there is a lot of fragmentation in the Android ecosystem—with many phones and versions of the operating system floating around—the similarities between these platforms are strong. And overall, even if users might change phones every two years, the new platform is likely to be fairly similar to the old one (unless, of course, they move from a feature phone to a smartphone).

- JavaScript still crashes, but most websites and apps do a good job of testing their products on mobile beforehand to make sure they work properly.

- Reluctance to use mobile shopping or spend money on mobile has slightly decreased. Although we definitely see more users willing to do it today than in 2009, the majority are still reticent to shop on mobile.

On the other hand, the download times are still a problem, even in the era of 4G. Also, the move by cellular carriers to charge by the megabyte makes users resent having to download too much, because they'll have to pay. And users still have the same kinds of difficulties in dealing with full sites on mobile: Although many of our participants are quite experienced mobile users, it doesn't seem to make a difference in their ability to navigate a full site. Last but not least, after a brief period of fading popularity, old media design seems to have come back in fashion, as the introduction of the iPad brought carousels, top navigation bars, and even print-like interfaces back in vogue.

The Nielsen Company is an independent company and is unaffiliated with any of us or with our company, Nielsen Norman Group. More about the survey cited in this section can be found at http://blog.nielsen. com/nielsenwire/ online_mobile/ state-of-the- appnation- %e2%80%93- a-year-of-change- and-growth-in-u-s- smartphones.

Usability Varies by Mobile Device Category

Our testing found three distinct classes of mobile UX, which are mainly defined by screen size:

- **Regular cellphones** with a tiny screen. Often called *feature phones*, these devices account for the majority of the world market (particularly in developing countries). They offer horrible usability, enabling only minimal interaction with websites.

- **Smartphones** (such as early BlackBerry models) in a range of form factors, typically with a midsize screen and a full A–Z keypad. These devices sometimes feature 3G Internet connectivity and perhaps even WiFi. Simple smartphones offer bad usability, forcing users to struggle to complete website tasks.

- **Full-screen phones** (such as iPhone, Android, and Windows Phone) with a nearly device-sized touch screen and a true GUI (graphical user interface) driven by direct manipulation and touch gestures. These phones offer 3G or better Internet connectivity and even faster speeds when connecting through WiFi. They offer the best usability among all different types of phones, but the experience is still often suboptimal. Typically users are successful when using a search engine to land on a deep page in a full site, or when they are on well designed sites or apps that are optimized for mobile.

Unsurprisingly, the bigger the screen, the better the user experience when accessing websites. Across several user testing studies done between 2009 and 2012, the average success rates between touch phones and smartphones were 20 percentage points (**Table 2.1**).

Table 2.1 Task Success Rates for Different Phone Types Across User Testing Studies 2009–2012

Phone	Success Rate
Feature phones	44%
Smartphones	55%
Touch phones	74%

With these numbers, the consumer advice is easy: Buy a touch phone if using websites is important to you.

The advice for Internet managers is more difficult. Considering the horrible usability of feature phones, should you even support them? Alternatively, should you focus on smartphone and touch phone users who are more likely to use your site extensively? There's no single answer.

For services highly suited for mobile use—such as news or social networking—you should probably create a dedicated feature-phone site, as well as a site optimized for higher-end phones. Most other websites might be better off concentrating their investment on a single mobile site optimized for touch phones. Also, if you focus on complex transactions or in-depth content, you'll probably have too few mobile users to justify a separate site.

In this book we are mainly concerned with touch phones. Unless we say otherwise, we're referring to a device like an iPhone or its competitors when we just use the term "phone." We'll explicitly use terms like "feature phone" when we want to discuss the more primitive devices.

There are three reasons we won't discuss the cheaper phones much in this book:

- Our research found that feature-phone usability is so miserable when accessing the Web that we recommend that most companies don't bother supporting feature phones.

- Empirically, websites see very little traffic from feature phones or smartphones, partly because people rarely go on the Web when their experience is so bad, and partly because the touch screen type of phone has seen a dramatic uplift in market share in recent years.

- Pragmatically, almost all participants in our training courses about mobile UX tell us that they don't design for simpler phones. The questions we get when we teach all relate to touch phones. We're betting that your interests, dear reader, will parallel those of our course participants.

A Separate Mobile Experience Is Best

For the best user performance, you should design different experiences for each mobile device class: The smaller the screen, the fewer the features, and the more scaled back your design should be. The very best option, at least in terms of user experience, is to go beyond browsing and offer a specialized downloadable mobile application for your most devoted users. In practice, however, an app is not an option for all sites.

Rich sites should build two mobile designs: one for low-end feature phones and another for big-screen phones. This strategy is especially good if you're targeting a broad consumer audience with many feature-phone users or if you're in a developing country. The small-phone experience is so different that it needs a dedicated and deeply scaled-back design, whereas the bigger phones benefit from a design that's mobile-friendly but not bare-bones. Feature-phone browsing is essentially a linear experience, whereas smartphone and full-screen browsing provide more of a GUI experience—albeit through a limited viewport.

(As mentioned earlier, our clients show no interest in feature-phone design, so we won't cover it more here. If you're one of the few companies that need a special site for feature phones, we strongly recommend that you run your own usability studies: The more primitive the user experience, the more important it is to get it exactly right.)

For most sites, however, the only realistic option is to supplement the main site with a single mobile site, recognizing that it will serve plain cellphones poorly. This strategy often makes sense. After all, most low-end mobile users suffer such misery when they attempt to visit websites that they do so for only the most compelling tasks, and thus might not use your site anyway. So, if you have only one mobile site, target the higher-end devices, as opposed to making a WAP-like site that everybody will hate.

WAP

Although many people may have heard the acronym WAP, few probably know that it stands for Wireless Application Protocol. It is a standard used by feature phones to display Web pages. Although when it was introduced (back in 1997) it made Web interactions possible on mobile and was perceived as empowering, WAP-style sites were fairly simple and characterized by lists of hyperlinks and plain text. Today WAP use has become obsolete and is limited to older feature phones. None of the modern smartphones make use of it.

In addition, not all sites need mobile versions. According to a diary study we conducted with users in six countries, people use their phones for a fairly narrow range of activities. So, because many mainstream websites won't see a lot of mobile users, they should just adapt their basic design to avoid the worst pitfalls for those few mobile users they'll get.

If your service makes sense for mobile users, offer at least one mobile-optimized design. If your site has a mobile design and a desktop design, serve the mobile version to all mobile users—even those with phones that support full-page browsing. (For users who need rare features that aren't in the mobile design, you should offer an easy way to switch to the full site.)

Mobile Site vs. Full Site

In a study we conducted in 2009, when our test participants used sites that were designed specifically for mobile devices, their success rate averaged 64 percent, which is substantially higher than the 53 percent recorded for using "full" sites—that is, the same sites that desktop users see.

Improving user performance is reason enough to create mobile-optimized sites. Such sites were also more pleasant to use and thus received higher subjective satisfaction ratings. This fact offers an additional rationale: When users are successful and satisfied, they're likely to come back.

We repeated this research in 2011, thinking that user performance might have gotten better. The success rate for mobile sites remained at 64 percent, whereas the success rate for full sites had increased to 60 percent. Obviously, full sites had become more mobile-friendly as companies became increasingly interested in supporting mobile users. Still, the main conclusion remained the same: Users were more successful when using sites that were optimized to be used on mobile devices.

The main guidelines for mobile-optimized websites are clear:

- Build a separate mobile-optimized site (or *mobile site*) if you can afford it. When people access sites using mobile devices, their measured usability is much higher for mobile sites than for full sites.

- A mobile app might be even better—at least for now, as discussed in the following section.

- If mobile users arrive at your full site, make sure they see your mobile site instead. Unfortunately many search engines still don't rank mobile sites high enough for mobile users, so people are often (mis)guided to full sites instead of the mobile ones, which offer a vastly superior user experience.

- Offer a clear link from your full site to your mobile site for users who end up at the full site despite the redirect. Make sure that the link labeled "Mobile" does not take users to a desktop page discussing your mobile offerings, as in *National Geographic's* case shown in **Figure 2.6**. When users type "nationalgeographic. com" into the mobile browser URL bar (or when they access the site through a search engine), they are taken to the full site instead of being redirected to *National Geographic's* mobile site. The top navigation bar of the full site contains a link titled "Mobile," but should mobile users click that, they are taken to a desktop-formatted page containing information about *National Geographic's* mobile site.

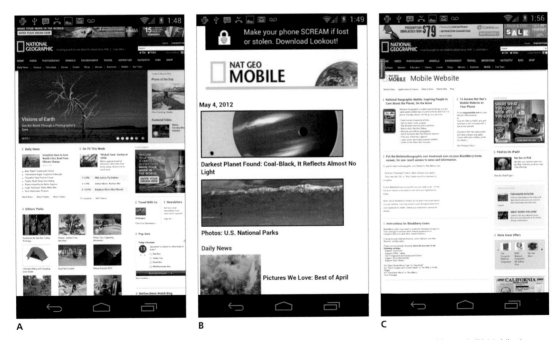

Figure 2.6 (**A**) *National Geographic's* full site (www.nationalgeographic.com). (**B**) Mobile site (m.nationalgeographic.com). (**C**) Page corresponding to the "Mobile" category in the top navigation bar.

Figure 2.7 Links from the mobile to full site: (**A**) Wikipedia (m.wikipedia.org) and (**B**) Yelp (m.yelp.com). The mobile versions of these sites contain a link to the full site at the bottom of the page.

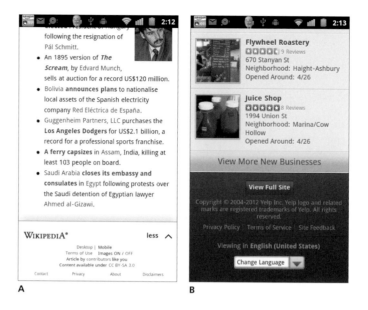

A   B

The label for the link to the full site can be either "Full site" or "Desktop (site)." "Desktop" is slightly more explicit, because some users may be confused by the terminology "full site."

- Offer a clear link from your mobile site to your full site for those (few) users who need special features that are found only on the full site (**Figure 2.7**). Most often that link can be placed at the bottom of the page.

The guidelines are different for large tablets (10-inch form factor, as in Apple iPad, Lenovo IdeaPad, Samsung Galaxy, etc.) where full sites work reasonably well. For small tablets (7-inch form factor, as in Amazon Kindle Fire) the ideal would be to create yet a third design optimized for midsize devices, although most companies can get away with serving their mobile site to Kindle Fire users.

Mobile-optimized Sites

The basic ideas for designing mobile-optimized sites are to:

- Cut features to eliminate functionalities that are not core to the mobile use case.

- Cut content to reduce word count and defer secondary information to secondary pages.

- Enlarge interface elements to accommodate the "fat finger" problem.

The challenge is to eliminate features and word count without limiting the selection of products. A mobile site should have less information about each product and support fewer tasks that users can do with the products, but the range of items should remain the same as on the full site. If users can't find a product on a mobile site, they assume the company doesn't sell it and go elsewhere.

In **Figure 2.8**, IKEA shows only one item under the Bed Frames category on its mobile website. Users are invited to "hurry" into a store to see more products. Limiting the selection of items on mobile makes the site unusable and is an example of poorly understood simplification for mobile. Especially on e-commerce sites, users should be able to find the same products on mobile and on the full site: The answer to a query or information should not vary depending on the platform on which the user is asking the question.

Figure 2.8 IKEA (m.ikea.com) shows a single product under the Bed Frames category on its mobile website and thus makes the site completely useless for mobile users.

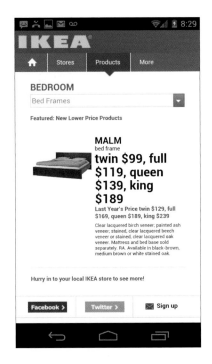

Similarly, a mobile real estate site should show all the homes for sale in a neighborhood, not just the ones most people are interested in buying. (Although it could offer a short list of popular houses as a shortcut so users could view them with a single touch.) But the mobile site could eliminate esoteric features—such as a property's past sales history—and offer users who need these features a link to the info on the full desktop site.

Why Full Sites Don't Work for Mobile Use

It's common today to hear people argue the following: *Mobile users have increasingly high expectations* for what they should be able to accomplish on their phones, so eliminating content or features will inevitably disappoint some people. It's therefore better, the (flawed) argument goes, to serve the full site to everybody, including mobile users.

This analysis is flawed because it assumes that the only choice is between the full-featured desktop site and a less-featured mobile site. However, any mobile site that complies with the usability guidelines will provide links to the full site wherever features or content are missing, so users have access to everything when and if they need it.

The design challenge is to place the cut between mobile and full-site features in such a way that the mobile site satisfies almost all the mobile users' needs. If this goal is achieved, the extra interaction cost of following the link to the full site will be incurred fairly rarely.

True, we've seen some underpowered and poorly designed mobile sites that would hardly satisfy anybody's mobile needs. But bad design that misinterprets a guideline is no reason to throw the baby out with the bathwater and neglect the well documented guideline. (In fact, if miserable user interfaces were a reason to reject an entire design category, we wouldn't have the Web at all; there are plenty of virtually unusable websites around. But that doesn't mean that we can't design good sites by following the guidelines that bad sites violate.)

The correct analysis is as follows:

- For the vast majority of tasks, mobile users will get a vastly better user experience from a well designed mobile site than from the full site.

- For a small minority of tasks, mobile users will be slightly delayed by the extra click to the full site.

A big gain that's experienced often will comfortably outweigh a small penalty that's suffered rarely.

A second argument against the mobile site option is that you could just optimize the entire website for mobile in the first place. Then, giving mobile users the "full" site wouldn't cause them any trouble. Although true, this analysis neglects the penalty imposed on desktop users when you give them a design that's suboptimal for bigger screens and better input devices (see the sidebar "Mouse vs. Fingers as an Input Device"). If desktop users were a minute minority, this might be acceptable, but almost all websites get substantially more traffic (and even more business) from desktop users than from mobile users. So although we do want to serve mobile users, we can't neglect desktop users—who, after all, pay most of our salaries.

Here are a few of the more important differences between desktop and mobile:

- The content should be different: Shorter and simpler writing is required for the smaller screen because the lack of context reduces text comprehension.

  (Yes, people can read novels on a Kindle or other tablets, but that's mainly useful for simple fiction with a linear plot that's easy to follow. Reading business-oriented content or other nonfiction that requires higher levels of cognitive processing is more difficult on smaller screens.)

- In addition to text, other content formats should also be designed for the medium. For example, *small images should be cropped and zoomed* differently than large images to emphasize salient details. It's not enough to simply rescale a single image to fill the available space for a given screen size. (As an example, see our discussion in the section "Case Study: Optimizing a Screen for Mobile Use" in Chapter 3, "Designing for the Small Screen," on design iterations of an image representing a Korean pop group on a mobile screen.)

- The information architecture (IA) changes to defer secondary content to secondary pages on mobile devices (as discussed in Chapter 4, "Writing for Mobile").

- Interaction techniques change due to the differences between finger- and mouse-driven input (see the sidebar "Mouse vs. Fingers as an Input Device").

- The feature set is reduced in mobile to lower complexity and to fit on the smaller screen.

The basic point? The desktop user interface platform differs from the mobile user interface platform in many ways, including interaction techniques, how people read, context of use, and the plain amount of content that can be grasped at a glance. This inequality is symmetric: Mobile users need a different design than desktop users. But, just as much, desktop users need a different design than mobile users.

Mobile Is Less Forgiving than Desktop

As discussed in Chapter 4, we advise site owners to eliminate secondary material when writing for mobile users. Many tweets, blog postings, and other comments on our usability guidelines all expanded on this theme: *Yes, do cut the fluff from mobile content,* **but also cut secondary content when writing for desktop websites.**

Desktop computers (and laptops) mainly use a mouse for input. Mobile devices and tablets mainly use the human finger for input.

Yes, sometimes bigger computers have a trackball and laptop users also often use a trackpad for input. And there are even a few mobile devices that come with a stylus. But mice and fingers are the main input device for currently popular user interfaces. So let's consider their differences.

Table 2.2 shows a comparison between input devices. Light blue cells indicate which pointing device is superior for each of the dimensions rated.

Here are some important notes for the table:

- Homing time is the time required to move the hands from one input device, such as the keyboard, to another, such as the mouse.
- Accelerated movements are the ability to have a nonlinear relationship between the speed of moving the pointing device and the onscreen pointer: Moving the mouse fast makes the onscreen pointer move even faster. Conversely, moving the mouse slowly makes the pointer move *very* slowly, allowing for high-precision pointing.
- When we say that there's virtually no learning time required to operate a touch screen by pointing a finger, we are assuming that users have already acquired sufficient dexterity in using their hands and fingers. This does take babies a few years.

The main takeaway from the table is that there is no single winner. Mice and fingers each have their strong points.

When designing a UI for a given platform, it's important to emphasize the strengths of the available input (and output) devices and also to work to alleviate their weaknesses.

For example, because the mouse has a hover state, tool tips and other roll-over effects can often be used to good effect on desktop computers. Similarly, context menus are easily supported by the two-button activation controls. These design elements are less natural on touch screens.

The fact that the mouse and touch input have such different strengths is one of the main reasons to design different UIs for desktop websites and for mobile sites (and also for desktop applications versus mobile apps).

Further arguments for two UIs are provided by the presence of a real keyboard on the desktop (making typing much faster and less error prone) and the vast difference in screen sizes.

Table 2.2 A Comparison Between Mouse and Fingers as Input Device

	Mouse	Fingers
Precision	High	Low
Number of points specified	1	Usually 1; 2–3 with multitouch
Number of controls	3: left/right button, scroll wheel	1
Homing time?	Yes	No
Signal states	Hover, mouse-down, mouse-up	Finger-down, finger-up
Accelerated movements	Yes	No
Suitable for use with big desktop monitors (30-inch or more)	Yes, because of acceleration	No, due to arm fatigue
Visible pointer/cursor	Yes	No
Obscures view of screen	No; thus allowing for continuous visual feedback	Yes
Suitable for mobile	No	Yes; nothing extra to carry around
Direct engagement with screen and "fun" to use	No; an indirect pointing device	Yes
Accessibility support	Yes	No
Ease of learning	Fairly easy	Virtually no learning time

In one way, we can only agree. As discussed in our book *Eyetracking Web Usability* (Peachpit Press, 2009), conciseness is a key guideline when writing for the Web. People don't read a lot on the Web and leave in a few seconds if a site doesn't communicate its value clearly. These findings lead to more detailed guidelines, such as emphasizing the first two words of nanocontent (for example, headlines and search engine links).

So yes, cut the blah-blah from your desktop site.

However, there's still a difference between writing for the Web and writing for mobile:

- Desktop copywriting must be concise.
- Mobile copywriting must be *even more* concise.

The high-level guideline is the same: Reduce secondary info. The difference is one of degree—certain information that might be acceptable on a desktop site should be delegated to a secondary page or even removed from a mobile site or app.

Our original research on how people read on mobile devices used the example of sending users a coupon with a special offer. In the study, the best design presented fairly limited information on the first screen. To read "more about this deal" users had to tap a link. (We discuss this example in more detail in Chapter 4.)

In a desktop design, it would have been better to show all the information on the first screen and save users a click. Why this difference?

- Mobile screens are much smaller: Reading through a peephole increases cognitive load and makes it about twice as hard to understand text on a mobile device as on a desktop. Short-term memory is weak, so the more users have to remember after it scrolls off the screen, the worse they'll do.

- Mobile users are even more rushed than desktop users because of the mobile setting.

Both differences support the same recommendation: Be more severe when cutting text for mobile than for desktop.

A similar finding applies to the choice of functionality: The feature set should be much smaller for a mobile site than for a desktop site. For sure, desktop sites should offer as few features as possible. For every feature that's removed, there is one less opportunity for the UI to confuse users, which makes the remaining features easier to use.

But a mobile site should have even fewer features than the desktop site (hence the guideline to offer a link from the mobile site to the full site for users who need features that only the desktop site supplies). The mobile site should have only those features that make sense for the mobile use case. For example, a company's full site typically includes PR information and investor relations sections, but this info should be eliminated from the mobile site.

Your desktop IA should always feature a simple navigation space that avoids an overly deep hierarchy. But for mobile, the limited space makes it even more important to prevent user disorientation; you should thus reduce the navigation options, because you can't show full contextual information on every screen. (The screen space allocated to navigation on a typical desktop site is more than the entire screen of a typical smartphone, leaving no room for the content.) That is, your navigation structure should be even shallower in a mobile IA.

The Best Buy example in **Figure 2.9** suffers from an overly deep hierarchy: Before seeing any products, users looking for an iPad cover must navigate through a five-level IA. Because users are often impatient on the go, a quicker path to content would be preferable in this situation.

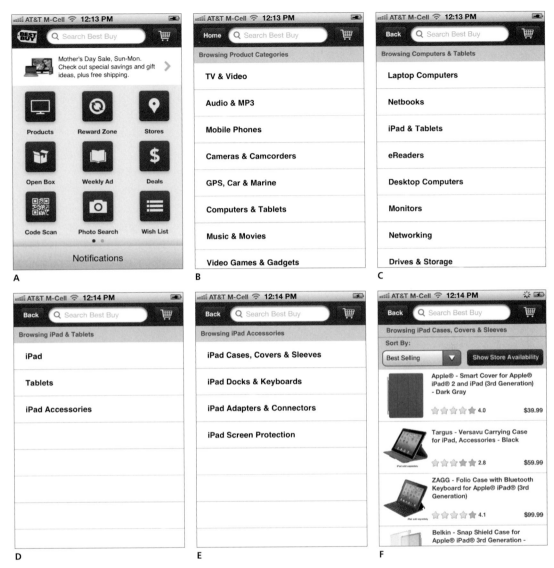

Figure 2.9 The Best Buy app for iOS features a too-deep information architecture. Thus, to see iPad covers, users need to navigate through the following hierarchy of pages: (**A**) "Products" page; (**B**) "Computers & Tablets" page; (**C**) "iPad & Tablets" page; (**D**) "iPad Accessories" page; (**E**) "iPad Cases, Covers, & Sleeves"; (**F**) Actual page listing the iPad covers.

Tablets form an intermediate case somewhere between phones and desktops, and are discussed further in Chapter 5, "Tablets and E-readers." Tablets' midsize screens allow for more context in writing and navigation than what fits on mobile screens, and also support richer features. On the other hand, the larger space encourages more complex gestures, which leads to its own usability problems.

Responsive Design

An increasingly popular way of dealing with the dilemma of full versus mobile sites is by using *responsive design*, which means optimizing the layout of a Web page for the screen dimensions and screen orientation. The different page elements are laid on a flexible grid; the grid morphs to the dimensions of the screen. Thus, the multicolumn layout in the desktop site becomes a single-column layout on mobile. The same content and site features are present in both the desktop and the mobile versions (**Figure 2.10**).

One of the advantages of responsive design is maintenance cost: Companies don't need to deal with two separate sites for desktop and mobile; instead, they can build a single site and make sure it looks right on the small screen. Also, responsive design better supports users whose mobile device is their only Internet access point (either because they might not own a computer or because they don't have access to one due to circumstances such as travel).

Responsive design can work well for those sites where all the features or content present on the full site are equally likely to be accessed on mobile. News (or newspaper) sites figure most prominently in this category: Because most features and content are equally likely to be accessed on mobile, it makes sense to serve a mobile-optimized version that's functionally equivalent with the full site (Figure 2.10).

Certain features make less sense on mobile than a desktop. For instance, a deep site hierarchy with multiple categories and subcategories might work on the desktop but may easily become a burden on mobile. Similarly, long lists of similar items can be difficult to scroll through on mobile if each item comes with a lot of details. (There is place for such details, but some could be delegated to a secondary page.)

In **Figure 2.11**, the "Working papers" page of the George Mason University School of Law shows at least two papers on the same desktop screen. In contrast, on mobile, a single paper entry (which includes the abstract) can take multiple screens. Even on a big-screen phone, such as a Samsung Galaxy Nexus, users must scroll for several pages to see the next paper. On mobile, a compressed abstract would be more effective and would enable users to quickly scan to the paper(s) of interest.

Figure 2.10 The *Boston Globe* (bostonglobe.com) on two different platforms: (**A**) on a desktop and (**B**)–(**C**) on an Android phone. The *Boston Globe* was one of the first sites to use responsive design.

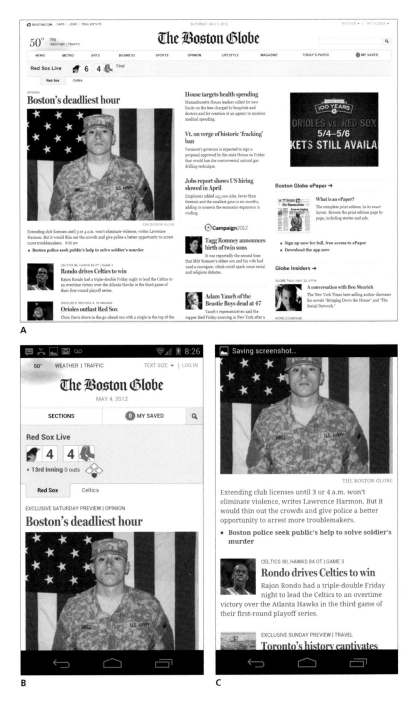

Figure 2.11 George Mason University School of Law (law.gmu.edu) is also a responsive-design site. Here you see the same page on different platforms: (**A**) a desktop screen shot of the "Working papers" page and (**B**)–(**C**) mobile screen shots of the same page. On mobile, users need to scroll a lot to get to the next paper.

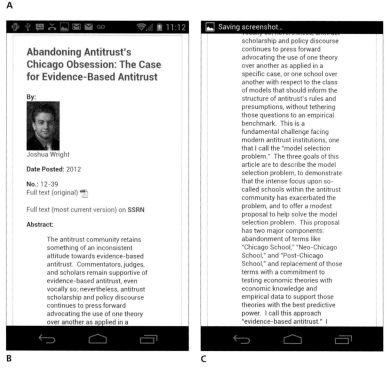

Mobile Usability

When considering mobile phones versus desktop computers, the platform differences are great enough that the benefits of creating two separate designs are substantial. In addition, both platforms have many wealthy users, so the profits from maximizing conversion rates can be considerable.

Still, the question remains whether the cost–benefit analysis truly supports two sites, or whether it would be more profitable to stick with a single site.

You must first consider your organization's size and how much business you conduct with mobile and desktop users. Some companies are so small that a higher conversion rate wouldn't translate into enough money to pay for two designs. Others might provide services that are targeted solely to mobile or desktop users and thus wouldn't suffer much from a lower conversion rate among the few users on the opposite platform. Also, if traffic is uniformly distributed across the site and budget is limited, a responsive design may be a good-enough solution.

Even if your organization is big enough to profit from separate mobile and desktop designs, some people claim that the cost is too high and that responsive design may be preferable instead.

However, responsive design isn't free in terms of interaction design or in terms of coding and implementation. For some sites, it might be cheaper than other implementation strategies; if that's true for you, then do go that route.

But the most important point is that responsive design—if done correctly—does involve creating distinct UIs for each platform. After all, the entire idea is that the design adapts (or "responds") to the capabilities of the user's specific platform.

In fact, responsive-design sites place on a continuum of mobile-specific customization. Many of them go beyond layout in customizing the mobile variant and do at least a minimum amount of content tuning on mobile: For instance, in the *Boston Globe* example (Figure 2.10), the topic names in the navigation bar are all collapsed under a single category called "Sections." Other sites, such as Pro-Publica (**Figure 2.12**), go even further by cutting out features that are less used on mobile.

Figure 2.12 ProPublica (propublica.org) uses responsive design. Here you see the same site on two different platforms: (**A**) on a desktop and (**B**) on a mobile device. The designers have gone beyond layout in customizing the mobile variant. Thus the top secondary navigation bar is absent on mobile, and fewer categories are in the main navigation bar: "Tools and Data" from the desktop is absent on mobile; "Our investigations" is renamed "Projects" on mobile (presumably to make better use of the limited space). Also note that just the project names are shown on mobile, whereas a short summary of the project appears on the desktop site.

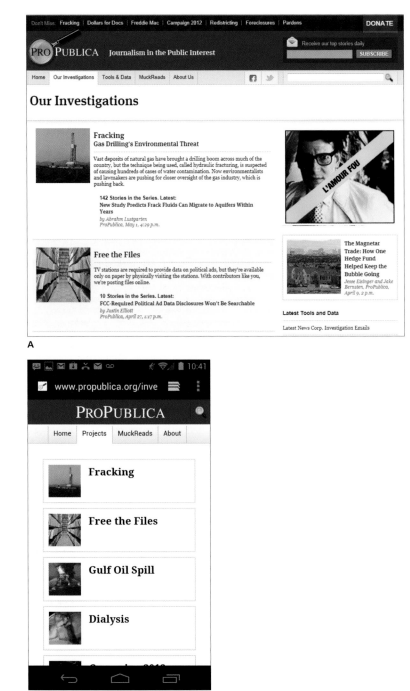

A

B

Most responsive-design examples that we've seen are fairly primitive and don't go far enough to create the sufficiently distinct UIs that mobile versus desktop use requires. It's not enough to simply modify the layout by moving content around on the screen and enlarging or diminishing particular design elements. This works only for adapting a desktop design to 19- versus 24-inch monitors, or for a mobile design for an iPhone versus a Kindle Fire.

As discussed in the previous section, mobile versus desktop design differences go far beyond layout issues. With enough coding, these differences can be supported through responsive design. In fact, you could argue that a design isn't responsive enough if it doesn't accommodate all the salient platform differences. However, once you do account for all the differences, we're back to square one: two separate designs.

Usability Guidelines Are Rarely Dichotomies

People want us to give hard and fast rules: Don't show more than X menu items; don't write more than Y words per page; nothing should be more than Z clicks from the homepage. Unfortunately UI design doesn't work that way. Usability questions seldom have a single answer. Rather, they are qualitative issues that specify the direction and nature of inevitable design trade-offs.

Every time your Web page's response time increases by 0.1 seconds, you'll lose a few percent of your visitors. But it's not true that *everybody* will wait 10 seconds, whereas *nobody* will wait 11 seconds.

As another example, consider the guideline about concise writing. The most concise copy would be a word or two, but that would typically make for an unsatisfactory Web page. In fact, sometimes longer articles can be better (although even in-depth articles should cut the fluff and be written at an appropriate comprehension level for their target audience).

The simple point remains: It's best to squeeze the text when writing for the Web. When you're writing for mobile, simply squeeze that orange even more. When you're considering which secondary content to defer to secondary pages, you need to move the cut-off point between primary and secondary when targeting mobile users. The principle remains the same, but your judgment should be harsher for mobile.

In all areas of user experience—feature set, IA, writing, images, and more—mobile usability requires stricter and more scaled-back design than desktop usability. That's why you need a separate mobile site. Simply using responsive Web design to make the full site accessible on mobile devices often results in a substandard mobile UX.

Mobile Sites vs. Apps: The Coming Strategy Shift

The most important question in a company's mobile strategy is whether to do anything special for mobile in the first place. Some companies will never get substantial mobile use and should stick to making their desktop sites less insufferable on small screens.

But if your site happens to have decent appeal to mobile users, the second strategy question is: Should you produce a mobile website or develop special mobile apps? The answer to this question today is quite different from what it will likely be in the future.

Current Mobile Strategy: Apps Best

As of this writing, there's no contest: Ship mobile apps if you can afford it. Our usability studies with mobile devices clearly show that users perform better with apps than with mobile sites. We measured a success rate of 74 percent when people used mobile apps, which is much higher than the 64 percent recorded for mobile-specific websites. (Mobile sites have higher measured usability than desktop/full sites when used on a phone, but mobile apps score even higher.)

The empirical data is really all you need to know. It's a fact that apps beat mobile sites in testing. To plan a mobile strategy, you don't need to know *why* the winner is best, but we'll try to explain it anyway.

Mobile applications are more usable than mobile-optimized websites because only limited optimization is possible during website design. An app can target the specific limitations and abilities of each device much better than a website can while running inside a browser. Beyond customization for the device, part of the secret of apps' success is that they tend to be simpler than sites, and often they can be boiled down to one to two easily accessible functionalities. When more features are crammed into an app, the complexity of the interface increases—and so does the likelihood of user failure.

Native application superiority holds for any platform, including desktop computers. However, desktop computers are so powerful that Web-based applications suffice for many tasks.

In contrast, mobile devices provide an impoverished user experience: tiny screens, slow connectivity, higher interaction cost (especially when typing, but also due to users' inability to double-click or hover), and less precision in pointing due to the "fat finger" problem. The weaker the device, the more important it is to optimize for its characteristics.

Apps can also provide a superior business case for content providers, because the various app stores offer a pseudo-micropayment ability that lets you collect money from users, which is harder to achieve over the public Internet.

Additionally, let's consider the differences between Nielsen's Law for Internet bandwidth and Moore's Law for computer power. Over the next decade, Internet bandwidth will likely become 57 times faster, and computers will become 100 times more powerful.

In other words, the relative advantage of running native code instead of downloading Web pages will be twice as big in ten years, which is one more point in favor of mobile apps.

Future Mobile Strategy: Sites Best

In the future, the cost-benefit trade-off for apps versus mobile sites will change.

Although we just said that computers will become 100 times more powerful, this doesn't necessarily mean that the iPhone 15 will be 100 times faster than the iPhone 5. It's more likely that hardware advances will be split between speed and other mobile priorities, especially battery lifetime. So, a future phone might be only ten times faster (but will be thinner, lighter, and able to run much longer between charges), whereas download times will be cut by a factor 57.

The expense of mobile apps will increase because there will be more platforms to develop for. At a minimum, you'll have to support Android, iOS, and Windows Phone. Also, many of these platforms will likely fork into multiple subplatforms that require different apps for a decent user experience.

For user experience purposes, iOS has already forked into iPad versus iPhone. Although they officially have the same OS software, the two devices need two very different designs.

Amazon.com's introduction of the Kindle Fire effectively forked the Android user experience with a fairly different platform. And you need a separate app with a separate UI to deliver decent usability on this nonstandard device. The 4.0 version of Android, Ice Cream Sandwich, was another fork: It replaced the physical buttons—Home, Back, Search, and Menu—present in earlier versions of Android with three virtual dimmable buttons—Home, Back, and Recent Apps (**Figure 2.13**).

Figure 2.13 The Amazon app on different versions of Android. (**A**) The older version of Android had four physical buttons. (**B**) The Kindle Fire has no physical buttons and instead uses virtual buttons that can be dimmed. (**C**) The latest version of Android, Android v. 4.0.2 (Ice Cream Sandwich), eliminated the physical buttons and replaced them with virtual buttons.

A

B

C

Physical buttons are real buttons that come as part of the hardware. The iPhone has one physical button (Home), and when Android first came out, up to the Android v.2.3.6 (Gingerbread), Android phones had four physical buttons (Back, Home, Menu, and Search).

In contrast, virtual buttons are part of the touch screen, and applications have the freedom to display them or dim them to reclaim the space for other content. The virtual buttons can change location to always be positioned at the bottom of the screen, whether the phone is in landscape or portrait orientation.

The Kindle Fire, which runs Amazon's version of Android, replaced the four physical buttons of older Android versions with virtual, or soft, buttons that can be dimmed by apps if they want to reclaim the corresponding screen space for other content. The latest version of Android, Android v. 4.0 (Ice Cream Sandwich), eliminated the physical buttons and replaced them with virtual buttons: Back, Home, Recent Apps, and (optional, depending on the app) Action Overflow. The Action Overflow button was intended to replace the Menu button in those apps that used it in prior Android versions (and thus ensure that these older apps would still be compatible with the newer OS version). The old physical Search button had a worse fate, because it had no equivalent in Ice Cream Sandwich. In addition, to increase the confusion, phone manufacturers that choose Android as their operating system have the option to include physical buttons (as Samsung did with its Galaxy SIII) or follow the official Google guideline and use virtual buttons.

In theory, physical buttons are an attractive concept: They can save precious screen real estate. You don't need to bother with interface widgets for Back and Search on the screen if you have dedicated physical buttons that do exactly that. The danger of physical buttons is that they typically are outside the user's visual focus of attention, and users must "think" about what these buttons might do and whether they may apply in the current situation, unless the function of these buttons is very consistent across contexts.

The trouble with the physical buttons in older Android versions is that people don't use them that much. With the exception of the Home and Back buttons, which are used heavily, the other buttons (Menu and Search) are often ignored by users. Part of the reason is that these buttons are not used consistently by apps (some apps do not use them at all, following an iPhone-like design; others use them only for nonessential functionality), so users do not have clear expectations for them. For that reason, many apps already duplicate physical button functionality with visible interface widgets that are more salient to the users and more likely to capture their attention.

So Google's move to forgo physical buttons in Android 4.0 was in the right direction, especially for the Menu and Search functions, but for the wrong reason: It solves a problem that Google created when it developed its first Android version, namely that Google did not produce or enforce clear standards for the use of these physical buttons, and as a result, they were used in random ways that did not encourage user learning.

The story is somewhat different for the Back and Home buttons. Although the Back button is also overloaded in Android (it can mean cancel, back to a previous screen within an app, or back to the previous app), it's used fairly consistently across apps, and people have learned to use it and rely on it.

It's only realistic to expect even further UI diversity in the future, which will make it expensive to ship mobile apps. (Although companies often try to cut costs by producing a single design for every platform and then generating specific code for each platform they want to address, there are still significant costs associated with the development of native apps.)

Apps have other disadvantages compared to websites. First, the app content is less discoverable than similar content on the Web. Searching within (multiple) apps is often more difficult than doing a single search on the Web and picking deep pages with the exact information that the user is looking for. Currently, we know of no apps that search within other apps and land the users on deep pages within those apps.

Second, the apps are less discoverable than the Web content. For specific information needs (such as finding out when the library closes), users are more likely to perform a Web search than to look up an app in an app store, download it, and then figure out if it contains the answer to their query. Users must work more to install a specific app, and even if they are willing to do it, they must know of the app in advance or be willing to spend the time to research it. For many tasks that require a quick, contextual answer, it will be faster to resort to the Web.

In contrast, mobile sites will retain some cross-platform capabilities, so you won't need as many different designs. High-end sites will need three mobile designs to target phones, midsize tablets (like the Kindle Fire), and big tablets. Using ideas like responsive design will let you adapt each of these site versions to a range of screen sizes and capabilities. The same basic UI design will work for a 6.8-inch tablet and a 7.5-inch tablet if you simply shrink or stretch the layout a bit. (A 5-inch phone would require a fundamentally different design—not just a modified layout—with fewer features and abbreviated content.)

Most important, new Web technologies, such as HTML5, will substantially improve mobile site capabilities. We're already seeing *mobile Web apps*—mobile sites with UIs that are very similar to native apps (**Figure 2.14**).

Today publishers, such as *Financial Times* and *Playboy*, use Web apps instead of apps for business reasons, not UI reasons. Publishers are tired of having a huge share of subscription revenues confiscated by app store owners, and *Playboy* wants to publish more titillating content than Apple's prudish censors allow.

Figure 2.14 Web apps work in the browser but look like native apps. (**A**) The *Financial Times'* Web app (app.ft.com). *Financial Times* decided to withdraw its native app for iPhone from the Apple App Store to circumvent subscription fees and be able to gather data on its subscribers. (**B**) OpenAppMkt (openappmkt. com) is a Web app that lists websites and Web apps. The tab bar at the bottom is similar to that encountered in native apps.

Freedom from censorship and the freedom to keep your own money are good reasons to stay with the free Internet instead of the walled garden of proprietary app stores. In the future, better UIs and more adaptive implementations will be additional reasons to go with mobile websites.

Another benefit of a mobile-site strategy is better integration with the full Web. It's much easier for others to link to a site than to integrate with a third-party application. In the long run, the Internet will defeat smaller, closed environments.

(Apps may remain better for tasks that are intensely feature-rich applications, such as photo editing, whereas mobile sites will be better for design problems like e-commerce/m-commerce, corporate websites, news, medical info, social networking, and so on that are rich in content but don't require intense data manipulation.)

When Will the Strategy Shift Happen?

Now for the $64,000 question—or more accurately for most companies, the million-dollar question: *When will the recommended strategy change?* In other words, when will the changeover in favor of mobile sites be strong enough for you to abandon mobile apps?

In the mobile realm, you'll often hear terms like *native app* or *Web app* or even *hybrid app*. What's the difference?

Native apps live on the device and are installed through an application store (such as Google Play or Apple's App Store). They are developed specifically for one platform and typically follow that platform's UI conventions. Users access them through icons on the device's home screen.

Web apps (Figure 2.14) are run by a browser. Users first access them as they would access any Web page: They navigate to a special URL and then have the option of "installing" them on their home screen by creating a bookmark to that page. They are typically platform-specific, because different browsers support different versions of HTML5 (the language of choice for these Web apps). They look and feel like native apps, but compared with the native apps, they are more limited in the kinds of phone features that they can access (for instance, they have more limited gesture support).

Hybrid apps (Figure 2.15) are native apps that use a browser within an app. They are installed in the same way as native apps (through an app store), but parts of the app render published Web pages. Often companies build hybrid apps as wrappers for an existing Web page, because they hope to get a presence in the app store without spending significant effort for developing a different app.

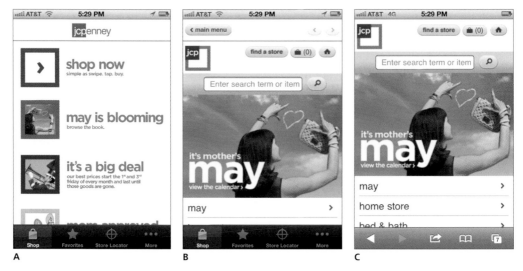

A   B   C

Figure 2.15 JC Penney's iPhone app is an example of a hybrid iPhone app. (**A**) The app has multiple sections. (**B**) The "Shop Now" section in the app contains a browser that shows the JC Penney mobile website. (The app page also displays the app-specific tab bar at the bottom and navigation bar at the top.) (**C**) The mobile page of JC Penney (m.jcpenney.com) accessed in the Safari browser.

Unfortunately, we don't know. Usability insights can tell us what's best for users under various circumstances, but they can't predict how fast these circumstances will change in the real world. In our experience, change comes more slowly than one might expect.

To conclude, we do believe mobile sites will win over mobile apps in the long term. But when that will happen is less certain. Today, if you are serious about creating the best possible mobile UX, our advice is to develop apps.

Mobile Apps

The "master guideline" for mobile apps is the same as that for all user interface design: Don't port a UI from an old interface paradigm to a new one. In the past this meant not slapping a GUI on top of something that was inherently a clunky mainframe flow. Now it means not adding touch-screen access to a desktop-oriented direct manipulation design. Users can't touch as precisely as they can click, so the number of manipulable graphical objects should be much fewer (so that each one can be much bigger).

Despite usability weaknesses in some apps, the main conclusion from watching mobile app users is that they suffered much less misery than users in our mobile website tests. In fact, testing people using mobile apps produced happier outcomes than testing people attempting to use websites on the same phone.

On mobile devices, applications are easier to use than websites.

Why are apps better than sites for mobile? Because the more impoverished the device, the more the design must be optimized for the platform's exact capabilities instead of bowing to a cross-platform common denominator.

Mobile Apps Are Intermittent-use Apps

A very strong conclusion from our user research is that people install many more apps than they actually use.

In the first part of each session, we asked users to walk us through their own mobile apps. We frequently heard comments such as, *"I downloaded this because [it sounded cool/a friend recommended it], but I haven't had time to try it."* Users also often said something like, *"I used this a few times right after I downloaded it, but I'm not using it anymore. I just haven't gotten around to deleting it."*

Web applications differ from traditional applications in several ways, and users view them as low-commitment transient encounters—a concept we refer to as *ephemeral use*.

An example of a Web-based ephemeral app would be the customization and configuration utilities often found on car sites. For such apps, users have zero commitment and arrive at the first screen with no knowledge of the functionality beyond what they may have gleaned from passing through previous pages on that site. (And we all know how little users read during most website visits.)

A Web-based application is usually a website component, meaning that users must navigate from a traditional, information-oriented Web page to the application's functionality-oriented tool. In our research of websites with embedded applications, users failed to make this initial step 36 percent of the time.

Once users find the application, they must understand what it does and what it can accomplish for them, as well as its general task flow and structure. This is true for all software, but most traditional software includes initial training that establishes the basics. Also, many software products are well known and users know their basic purpose even before installing them. This is true for enterprise systems (such as intranet-based expense reporting or time sheets) and desktop software (such as PowerPoint). In contrast, users are thrown directly into an embedded application from the website, often unexpectedly.

Users have less motivation to understand advanced features in website-embedded applications, because the applications are not typically a core part of their work. In contrast, many jobs demand traditional software use, either as a defining aspect of someone's work (as with airline reservation agents, for example) or to generate the deliverables that measure employee performance (as is often the case with Microsoft Office).

Users rarely return to the same Web application multiple times, so they'll rarely benefit from a buildup of learning about a specific GUI. In contrast, traditional software is often used repeatedly by the same person.

If you can get people to use your mobile app repeatedly, you have a great advantage relative to these embedded applications that live within websites. However, as discussed in the main text, that's a big if, because users often download apps without using them very much.

The first conclusion from this finding is that pure download numbers are obviously irrelevant. To measure your app's success, you must measure actual use. And to assess whether you're really meeting user needs, you must go even further and measure sustained use. If people use an app a few times and then give up on it, you have a failed mobile design on your hands.

A few mobile apps do get frequent use, ranging from Facebook to the Weather Channel. But most businesses can't realistically aspire to enter this category. Mobile apps have different usability criteria than core desktop-productivity applications, as well as the mission-critical enterprise software that people use every day on the job.

Mobile mainly equals intermittent use. This does indicate a deeper level of user commitment than the ephemeral applications we often study on websites.

Mobile apps score a little better than ephemeral website apps, because users actively decide to install them. This creates a *minimum level of commitment* to explore the app—although, as we found, this level is often very low indeed. Still, it's higher than zero.

The second conclusion from this finding is that because the app icon is a *continuous presence* on the phone, it acts as a tiny voice gnawing at the user to try it out. Again, this isn't a very strong force; humans are great at selective attention. Basically people tune out anything they don't really want to pay attention to, so users' eyes pass by unused icons very quickly. Plus most users have lots of apps on their phones, and it's likely that any particular app icon can get lost in the sea of similar icons. And, at least on iOS, app icons can get buried in folders (**Figure 2.16**) and never retrieved again.

These are simply facts of the overall mobile UX: An app is easy to download from an application store, and social pressure causes many "fun" apps to migrate quickly through large user pools. As a result, the app launching pages quickly become polluted with frivolous icons that people don't really need and don't use after leaving the bar or pub that evening.

Figure 2.16 Folders on iOS: Each folder hides several apps. Downloading an app does not guarantee that the user will use it. As apps get buried on multiple application screens and in folders, users often forget about having installed them. There is a long tail distribution of application usage: A few apps (Mail, Weather, Facebook, favorite games) get used a lot, but most apps are used rarely if ever.

If you're designing a "serious" business app that you think offers real benefits to your customers, you might feel above the fray of rude, bodily noise apps. But you're not. Readers of the old book *Designing Web Usability* (Peachpit Press, 1999) might recall Jakob's Law of the Web User Experience: Users spend most of their time on *other* sites (than your site). Your website is part of the Web ecosystem, and your site's usability is dictated by the overall Web user experience, which is dominated by the sum of all other sites people visit.

When you're posting business information on social media sites, for example, that information has to live within your followers' personal space, which is constructed by their family and real friends. Similarly, your app is a small part of the total app user experience.

Fair or not, that's life. Deal with it. Design for it.

Half-speed Progress, But Hope Ahead

Our first study of mobile usability was conducted in 2000, and the conclusion then was that mobile Web 2000 = desktop Web 1994. (See the Appendix, "A Bit of History," for a summary of this early research.)

In a study we conducted in London in 2009, we repeated two tasks from our study of WAP usability in 2000. We expected to find reasonable improvements in task performance, but the results contradicted those expectations (which is obviously why we bother doing research). The mean task times from the two studies are shown in **Table 2.3**.

Table 2.3. Mean Task Times in 2000 and 2009

Task	WAP Phones (2000)	Modern Phones (2009)
Find the local weather for tonight	164 sec.	247 sec.
Find what's on BBC TV 1 tonight at 8 p.m.	159 sec.	199 sec.

Amazingly, users spent 38 percent more time on these two tasks in 2009 than they did in 2000. Are modern mobile devices really worse than the horrible WAP phones of times past? Has site usability declined that much? The answer is *no* on both counts: Phones and sites are definitely better now.

What has changed is the *usage environment*. In 2000, users were restricted to the "walled garden" supplied by their mobile carrier. WAP phones came with a built-in "deck" that supplied direct access to a few selected services. Although this approach limited users' freedom and restricted them to only the simplest of tasks, they could get to the information with just a few key presses.

Today's mobile users are highly search-dominant. When we don't specify which site or app they should use (and often even when we do), they turn first to their favorite search engine. Again, this means plenty of typing, which is slow, awkward, and error prone on mobile devices.

Today mobile users can do anything. The fact that doing most tasks takes so long further emphasizes the need for scaled-back mobile site designs.

In our 2009 study, one user did very well—an iPhone user who used a weather app to get the weather forecast in only 18 seconds (one-third of the fastest speed from 2000). If any additional evidence were needed for mobile-dedicated design's benefits, this example should surely suffice.

In our most recent mobile user research, users' average success rate was 62 percent. This is only three percentage points better than the mobile usability score we had recorded three years previously. Although this improvement rate might seem disappointingly slow, it's about the same as the pace we recorded for desktop Web use in 263 studies over the last 12 years.

Observing users accessing websites on their mobiles in 2009 reminded us of testing wired users in 1998. In other words, during the nine-year period from 2000 to 2009, we've seen four years' worth of progress in mobile user experience. Roughly speaking, improvements in mobile usability moved at half the pace of wired usability.

During the last four years mobile UX improved at a much faster pace, and the usability of using high-end phones in 2012 was probably similar to that of using desktop websites in 2004. It's still much harder to get tasks done on a phone than on a desktop computer, but not as difficult as it used to be.

The rate of improvement probably doubled with the increased competition of multiple touch-screen platforms (iPhone, Android, Windows Phone, etc.) and with the profusion of mobile sites and apps.

So why are we still bullish on mobile websites and online services?

We have turned a corner in mobile Web usability. Just as Apple's Macintosh heralded a breakthrough in personal computer usability in 1984, its iPhone pioneered a similar breakthrough in mobile usability after 2007.

The iPhone is certainly not perfect, and competitors could easily make better mobile devices. By "easily" we don't mean over a weekend. We simply mean that it's possible to do it given a strong focus on user experience and user-centered design: iPhone leaves a lot of ground for improvement. So far, however, iPhone competitors have been a bit behind—or if we're generous, we could say that they have matched iPhone's usability without surpassing it.

Alan Kay famously said that the Mac was "the first computer worth criticizing." Similarly, the iPhone was the first mobile Internet device worth criticizing. It's a starting point, not an end point, for mobile online-services access.

Although devices will get better, the big advances must come from websites. Sites (including intranets) must develop specialized designs that optimize the mobile UX. Today many sites still don't have mobile versions, and those that do are often poorly designed, lacking knowledge of the special guidelines for mobile usability.

Every year we run a design competition to identify the world's ten best-designed intranets. In 2009 we began seeing some good mobile intranet designs, with 30 percent of winning intranets having a mobile version. In 2011 the mobile space looked even more promising when this number doubled to 60 percent. But alas, in 2012 the number dropped to 10 percent; only Genentech offered mobile intranet design in its series of iOS apps (Apple was the dominant platform internally in this company). Other winners offered mobile intranet access to employees on the network but without optimizing for mobile.

There are three probable reasons for the lack of traction in the mobile intranet space:

- Intranet groups still don't have the budget and resources needed to develop mobile platforms.
- Unless the organization has one company-issued mobile device, it's difficult for intranet teams to choose which device to focus on. So instead they design for none.
- Creating a mobile intranet version that would work on any device is one possible solution. However, as discussed earlier in this chapter, even a single mobile version would have to be a separate design from that of the website to be truly helpful and usable for employees. And it takes resources to create and maintain two separate applications.

While we await more insights specifically about mobile intranets, a good first step would be to follow the usability guidelines for mobile websites and apps we discuss in this book. For other aspects of user experience, we usually find that intranet usability builds on top of Web usability: Intranet users also use websites and form many of their expectations from their experience with mainstream sites. The same is likely true for mobile design.

Thus although we don't specifically cover mobile intranets in this book, you can still benefit from the lessons if you're designing a mobile intranet.

3 Designing for the Small Screen

All of our research findings support a single conclusion: Designing for mobile is difficult. Technical accessibility is very far from providing an acceptable user experience. It's not enough that your site will display on a phone. Even touch phones that offer "full-featured" browsers don't offer PC-level usability in terms of users' ability to actually get things done on a website.

When you're designing for mobile, there's a tension between a) making content and navigation salient so that people don't have to work too hard to get there, and b) designing for a small screen and for slow downloading speeds. That's why almost every design decision must be made in the context of the site being designed, and what works for one site may not work for another.

Mobile users face four main usability hurdles:

- **Small screens.** For a device to be mobile, it must be easy to carry and thus relatively small. Small screens mean fewer visible options at any given time, requiring users to rely on their short-term memory to build an understanding of an online information space. This makes almost all interactions harder. It's also difficult to find room for multiple windows or other interface solutions that support advanced behaviors, such as comparative product research (**Figure 3.1**).

Figure 3.1 Best Buy's app for Android has a compare-products feature. You can compare at most four products at a time with two products visible at the same time on a screen. For these screen shots, we selected three GPS devices: (**A**) Comparison between item 1 and item 2 at the top part of the page. (**B**) Comparison between item 2 and item 3 at the top part of the page. (**C**) Comparison between items 2 and 3 continues as the user scrolls down.

The comparison table in Figure 3.1 requires a lot of scrolling, both horizontal and vertical, and puts significant demands on users' short-term memory. First, the comparison table effectively compares only two items (the ones next to each other in the comparison list): To compare items 1 and 3, users must keep a lot of information in their short-term memory and move back and forth between different screens. Second, because the table is long and spreads across several screens, users don't have all (or even most) of the features in front of them, so they still have to remember how the items fared on those dimensions that are relevant to them but not necessarily visible at the same time. In addition, in screen shot Figure 3.1C, the screen real estate is underutilized: A lot of empty space surrounds the text, plus the layout that alternates feature names with their values makes the table more difficult to scan.

- **Awkward input, especially for typing.** It's tricky to operate GUI widgets without a mouse: Menus, buttons, hypertext links, and scrolling all take longer and are more error prone, whether they're touch activated or manipulated with a teensy trackball. Text entry is particularly slow and littered with typos, even on devices with dedicated mini keyboards.

- **Download delays.** Accessing the next screen takes forever—often longer than it would on a dial-up connection, even with a supposedly faster 3G or 4G service.

- **Mis-designed sites.** Because websites are often optimized for desktop usability, they don't follow the guidelines necessary for usable mobile access.

The first two problems seem fundamental. Mobile devices will never offer screens as big or input devices as good as a full-fledged PC.

Connectivity problems will hopefully diminish in the future, but it will take many years until mobile connections are as fast as a good cable modem—let alone as fast as the broadband connections promised by wireline improvements.

Mobile will never be the same as desktop. So users are left with the hope that websites will be redesigned for better mobile usability.

Wasted Mobile Space

To have a successful mobile site or app, the obvious guideline is to design for the small screen. Unfortunately some designers don't, and we still see users struggle to tap tiny areas that are much smaller than their fingers. The "fat finger" syndrome will be with us for years to come.

The second point is more conceptual—and more difficult for some people to accept: For a device with a small screen, you must limit the number of features to those that matter the most for the mobile-use case.

Even on desktop computers, precious pixels are the world's most valuable real estate. Amazon.com's Add to Cart button is 160×27 pixels, or 0.003 square feet (0.0003 m^2) at a typical 100 dpi desktop monitor resolution. You could crowd almost 800,000 Buy buttons onto the floor space of the average American home, which currently sells for $160,000. Even a single Buy button will often bring in more than that—let alone the revenue from 800,000 buttons.

Normally, when something is extremely valuable, you try to conserve it. But screen space shouldn't be hoarded; it should be spent. We see too many designs that cram highly valuable content or action items into tiny spaces while wasting vast amounts of screen space.

Mobile screens are so small that it's a sin to waste space.

Figure 3.2 shows a screen from one of our iPad studies. The user interface to the current news is a huge sphere; you can spin it using gestures. It's a neat graphic, and the initial interaction is enticing: At first users found it *"kind of cool," "really cool," "fancy," "eye-catching,"* and *"kind of fun."*

Despite these positive initial reactions, users didn't like the screen and turned to an alternate view as soon as they discovered it (**Figure 3.3**). Regular users of the ABC app told us that they preferred the more standard-looking news listing as their main screen when using the app.

Why do users favor the regular, slightly boring design for everyday, actual use? Because it shows more news at a glance. The sphere offers a clear view of only a single story. Other stories have distorted images and captions that are hard-to-impossible to read. What a waste of screen space.

A second example comes courtesy of The Weather Channel app for iPad (**Figure 3.4**). The Weather Channel manages to waste the iPad's screen space by crowding most of the weather information in a narrow strip at the bottom of the screen and devoting the screen space to a purely generic decorative picture. Touching the screen does bring some extra information, but the default is disappointingly bare.

Figure 3.2 (Top Left) ABC News iPad app: home screen.

Figure 3.3 (Top Right) ABC News iPad app: The alternate home screen with more news. This is what people actually use.

Figure 3.4 (Bottom) This is such a bad use of space. The Weather Channel for iPad uses most of the iPad screen for a big, mostly irrelevant picture and the current temperature.

Almost always, two interfaces for the same dataset are too many. They usually indicate a lazy design: The designers weren't sure which of the two interfaces was the better one, so let the users decide.

The use of two interfaces or views for the data is justified only when the two views emphasize significantly different aspects of the data.

In **Figure 3.5**, iBooks and Yelp allow users to switch how they see their data: iBooks has a bookshelf and a list view, and Yelp has a list and a map view. While in Yelp's case, each of the two interfaces allows users to inspect different aspects of the data (type of restaurant and ratings in the list view; relative position with respect to a landmark in map view), in iBooks' case, one of the two interfaces is clearly superior to the other (and, unfortunately, it's not the default one). Indeed, the list view makes it easier for the user to parse the author and title of the book, or find any one book by title (because books are ordered alphabetically by title in this view but not in the bookshelf view). Although you can argue that the bookshelf view supports visual recognition of the book covers, as the number of books increases, the ability of recognizing a book by the cover decreases.

Figure 3.5 Alternate interfaces: iBooks and Yelp. (**A**) Bookshelf view for iBooks; (**B**) List view for iBooks; (**C**) List view for Yelp; (**D**) Map view for Yelp. Yelp's use of two interfaces is justified, whereas iBooks' is not.

Higher information density = less need to move around and greater likelihood that you see what you want.

Edward R. Tufte's call for charts with more "*data ink*" in his masterwork *The Visual Display of Quantitative Information* (Graphics Press, 2001) is related to this idea, although slightly different: Printed charts are different from interactive user interfaces (UIs). In a UI, you can't cram the screen full of too much info or users will feel overwhelmed.

In **Figure 3.6** Weather Bug attempts to increase the UI density and get some extra space 1) by using a carousel in the tab bar that contains the navigation options and 2) by not using labels for the icons in this tab bar. The result is arguably too complex. The icons in the tab bar at the bottom of the screen are too cryptic and have low information scent (see the sidebar "Information Scent"). Instead it would be better to use more standard OS icons, or at least supplement the icons with a text label. The carousel tab bar is an attempt to fit more options in a tab bar that typically accommodates only five items.

Figure 3.6 Weather Bug app for Android packs too much UI in a small space: (**A**) The first four icons of the carousel (at the bottom of the page) and (**B**) the rest of the icons in the carousel.

A   B

Chrome

What do we mean when talking about the chrome in a user interface design?

Chrome is the visual design elements that give users information about the screen's content or provide commands to operate on that content. These design elements are provided by the underlying system—whether it is an operating system, a website, or an application—and surround the data provided for the user.

Not coincidentally, Chrome is also the name of Google's Web browser, although we don't use the term in that sense here.

We don't know who came up with the term chrome, but it was likely a visual analogy with the use of metal chrome on big American cars during the 1950s: The car body (where you sit) was surrounded by shiny chrome on the bumpers, tail fins, and the like.

Similarly, in most modern GUIs, the chrome lives around the edges of the screen, surrounding the middle area, which is dedicated to the user's data.

Chrome at different system levels

The following are some examples of chrome, which vary depending on the "underlying system":

- On a **Windows PC** the chrome is the Windows operating system. In Windows 7 the chrome consists of the Start button, the task bar, the system tray, and the Recycle Bin. We might also consider the gadget area to be chrome, particularly if a user simply sticks to those gadgets that ship with the system (as many do, due to user inertia and the power of defaults).

- In **application software**, such as a word processor, the chrome is found in the menu bar, the ribbon or toolbars, rulers, scroll bars, and various specialized panes, such as Microsoft Word's thesaurus bar or Adobe Photoshop's palette of color swatches.

Tufte: The Data Display Genius

Edward R. Tufte has written a host of beautifully illustrated books about data display. The first of his books remains the best: *The Visual Display of Quantitative Information*, 2nd edition (Graphics Press, 2001).

You might think that a book from 2001 would be too old to help you design cutting-edge mobile user interfaces. You would be wrong. Although Tufte's examples are often centuries old, his principles for clearly communicating data visually are timeless.

Tufte's second-best book is *Envisioning Information* (Graphics Press, 1990). Because this book hasn't been published in a second edition, it's even older than his first book. But the recommendations are just as timeless.

- In a **Web browser** the chrome includes the URL field, browser toolbars, browser buttons, tabs, scroll bars, and status fields.

- In a **mobile app** the chrome often includes a status bar across the top of the screen and a tab bar with command icons across the bottom. Sometimes there's also a navigation bar below the status bar.

- On a **website** the chrome includes navigation bars, footers, logos, branding, the search box, and so forth.

Figure 3.7 shows some examples of chrome in mobile apps. In the Apple Store (Figure 3.7A), the tab bar and the search bar help users navigate the app but are not content. In Adobe Ideas (Figure 3.7B), the toolbar and the bar at the top are chrome, because they enable the user to act upon the file displayed.

Figure 3.7 Chrome in mobile apps. (**A**) In the Apple Store app for iPhone the tab bar at the bottom and search bar at the top are part of chrome. (**B**) In Adobe Ideas for iPhone, the toolbar on the side and the bar at the top are chrome. (Here you see a blank image, which makes the chrome particularly conspicuous.)

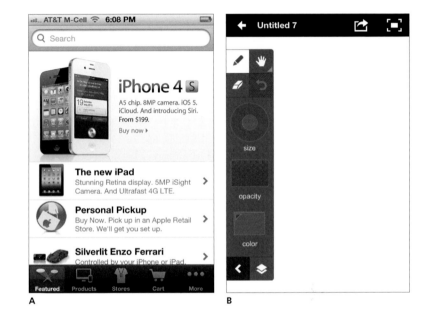

A   B

Chrome obesity: Don't eat my pixels

The penalty of chrome is clear: Chrome takes up screen space, leaving less for the target content or data. This is particularly bad on mobile devices where screen space is at an even higher premium than on tablets or PCs. But even on a 30-inch desktop monitor, the combined Windows and Microsoft Excel chrome means that users can see only 67 rows of data in a spreadsheet instead of the 80 rows that would theoretically fit on the screen. Thus without the chrome, people would be able to review about 19 percent more data.

The spreadsheet example shows another downside of chrome: It accumulates as systems are nested within layers of other systems, each with its own chrome. Because cumulative chrome often eats more than half of all pixels, one guideline is certainly to beware of chrome obesity.

A second guideline is to consider ways of temporarily hiding parts of the chrome and reveal it only when needed. Doing so is dangerous, however, because what's out of sight is often out of mind, and you definitely cannot rely on short-term memory in user interface design.

Chrome that comes and goes works only if you:

- Use a simple and reliable operation to reveal the chrome (don't use gestures that are abstruse or subject to accidental activation).

  Many content-intensive apps hide the chrome to maximize the screen space allotted to the actual content and make the experience more immersive (**Figure 3.8**). Users can expose the controls by tapping on the page.

  To make it clear to the user that the controls are accessible through the tap gesture, we recommend that, like Instapaper in Figure 3.8, the app start by showing the chrome and then hide it after the user has spent a few seconds on the page. We recommend using a slow fade-out to hide the chrome instead of having it disappear in a blink. This simple animation draws a bit of attention to the vanishing chrome (and thus should not be overdone).

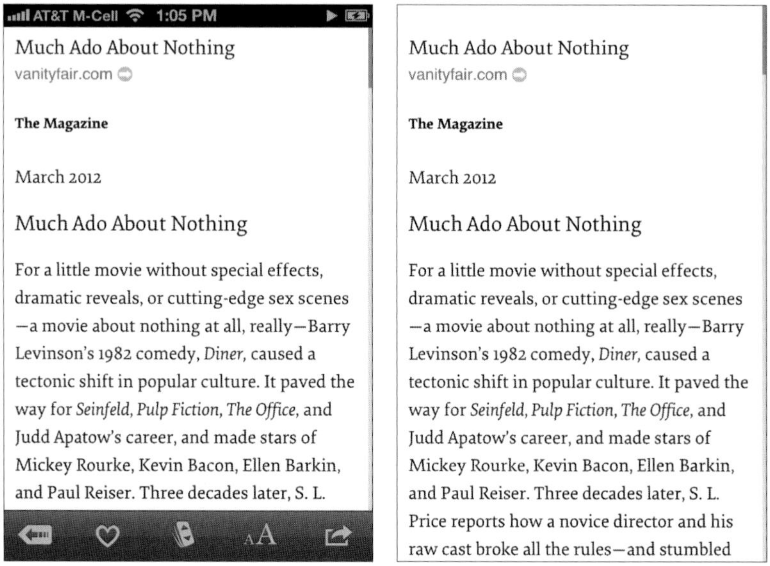

Figure 3.8 Instapaper app for iOS: (**A**) chrome exposed and (**B**) chrome hidden. Instapaper is an app that allows users to save articles from the Web and read them later at their leisure.

A

.ııll AT&T M-Cell 🛜 1:05 PM ▶ 🔋

Much Ado About Nothing
vanityfair.com ◎

The Magazine

March 2012

Much Ado About Nothing

For a little movie without special effects, dramatic reveals, or cutting-edge sex scenes —a movie about nothing at all, really—Barry Levinson's 1982 comedy, *Diner,* caused a tectonic shift in popular culture. It paved the way for *Seinfeld, Pulp Fiction, The Office,* and Judd Apatow's career, and made stars of Mickey Rourke, Kevin Bacon, Ellen Barkin, and Paul Reiser. Three decades later, S. L.

B

Much Ado About Nothing
vanityfair.com ◎

The Magazine

March 2012

Much Ado About Nothing

For a little movie without special effects, dramatic reveals, or cutting-edge sex scenes —a movie about nothing at all, really—Barry Levinson's 1982 comedy, *Diner,* caused a tectonic shift in popular culture. It paved the way for *Seinfeld, Pulp Fiction, The Office,* and Judd Apatow's career, and made stars of Mickey Rourke, Kevin Bacon, Ellen Barkin, and Paul Reiser. Three decades later, S. L. Price reports how a novice director and his raw cast broke all the rules—and stumbled

- Offer rock-solid consistency so that the hidden chrome's existence is drilled into the user's long-term memory through excessive repetition and the absence of any exceptions.

- Mitigate the complexity of hidden chrome by using *contextual tips* and *progressive disclosure* (see the sidebar "Progressive Disclosure"). The concept of progressive disclosure (often used in games to familiarize new players with the game) must be applied in this environment as well: Users need to be gently led by the hand and offered suggestions one at a time in the right context, when that information is truly useful, rather than being flooded with all the chrome information at the beginning and out of context.

Adobe Photoshop Express is a photo-editing app for iOS that effectively uses progressive disclosure via contextual tips (**Figure 3.9**). When users choose a menu option such as Sharpen, a tip tells them what gesture to use to sharpen the image. Users are shown the tip only when they are in the context where that tip can help.

Figure 3.9 Adobe Photoshop Express uses contextual tips to mitigate the lack of chrome: (**A**) When users choose Sharpen, a tip tells them what gesture to use to sharpen the image. (**B**) When the tip is dismissed, users can sharpen the image by sliding their finger on the screen. (The number at the top shows the current sharpening level.)

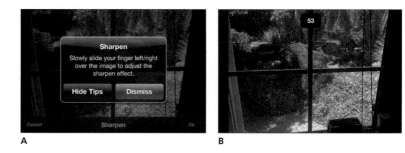

A   B

Gestures instead of chrome?

A common alternative to chrome on touch screens is using gestures to perform actions that normally are delegated to buttons. Gestures can work well provided that they have the right affordance and there are not too many. For instance, many book-reading (and other content-reading) apps use the swipe gesture for turning the page. They have eliminated the Back button and replaced it with the swipe gesture, localized on the left side of the page. The same swipe gesture moves to the next page when it is localized on the right. This gesture is fairly similar to that used for turning pages in a physical book, and most users discover it fairly quickly (**Figure 3.10**). However, the two-finger swipe used by some iPad magazines (such as *Popular Science*) to move to the next article doesn't have the same kind of affordance and is harder to discover (see the section "Low Memorability and Gestures" in Chapter 5, "Tablets and E-readers").

Interaction designers face the dilemma of fulfilling two contradictory requirements:

- Users want power, features, and enough options to handle all of their special needs. (Everybody is a special case somehow. For example, who wants line numbers in a word processor? Millions of users, that's who, including most big law firms.)
- Users want simplicity; they don't have time to learn a profusion of features in enough depth to select the few that are optimal for their needs.

Progressive disclosure is one of the best ways to satisfy both of these conflicting requirements. It's a simple yet powerful idea that can be achieved in two steps:

1. Initially show users only a few of the most important options.
2. Offer a larger set of specialized options upon request. Disclose these secondary features only if a user asks for them, meaning that most users can proceed with their tasks without worrying about this added complexity.

In a system designed with progressive disclosure, the very fact that something appears on the initial display tells users that it's important.

For novice users this helps prioritize their attention so they spend time only on features that are most likely to be useful to them. By hiding the advanced settings, progressive disclosure helps novice users avoid mistakes and saves them the time they would have spent contemplating features they don't need.

For advanced users, the smaller initial display also saves them time because they avoid having to scan past a large list of features they rarely use.

Progressive disclosure thus improves learnability, efficiency of use, and error rate.

You might assume that by initially focusing users' attention on a few core features, they might build a limiting mental model of the system and thus be unable to understand all of their options. Research says that these are groundless worries: People understand a system *better* when you help them prioritize features and spend more time on the most important ones.

Simple as the concept may seem, you must get two aspects right when designing for progressive disclosure:

- You must get the right split between initial and secondary features. You have to disclose everything that users frequently need up front, so they only have to progress to the secondary display on rare occasions. Conversely, the primary list can't contain too many options or you'll fail to sufficiently focus users' attention on truly important issues. Also, the initial display can't contain confusing features or you'll slow down user performance.
- It must be obvious how users progress from the primary to the secondary disclosure levels:
  - Make the mechanics of this operation simple, and place the advanced features button in a clearly visible spot.
  - Label the button or link in a way that sets clear expectations for what users will find when they progress to the next level. (In other words, the progression should have strong information scent.)

You may have noticed that these guidelines for progressive disclosure are very similar to our recommendations in Chapter 2 for how to distribute features between a mobile site and a full website. That's no coincidence, because the two-site strategy is simply one more example of progressive disclosure when accessed by a mobile user.

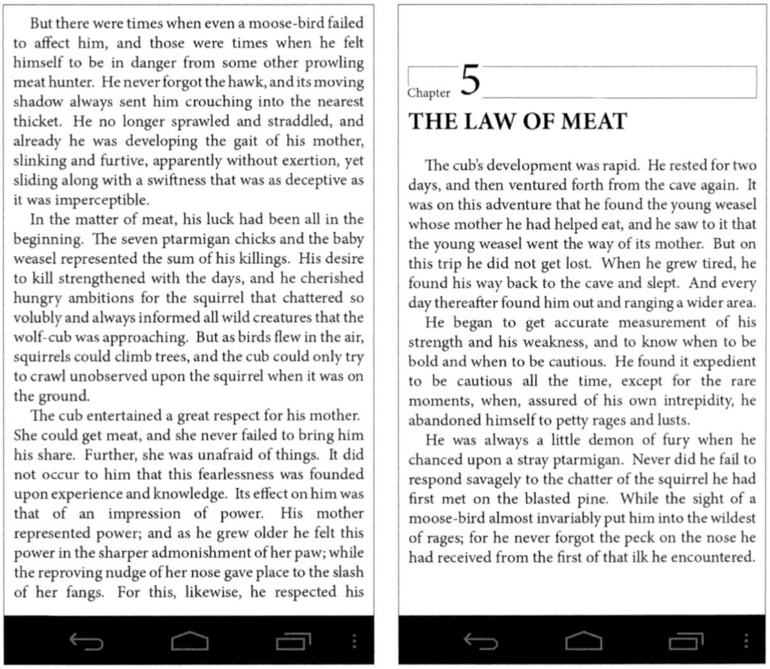

Figure 3.10 Aldiko app for Android: (**A**) Page in a book. (**B**) Swiping on the left moves to the previous page in the book.

But there were times when even a moose-bird failed to affect him, and those were times when he felt himself to be in danger from some other prowling meat hunter. He never forgot the hawk, and its moving shadow always sent him crouching into the nearest thicket. He no longer sprawled and straddled, and already he was developing the gait of his mother, slinking and furtive, apparently without exertion, yet sliding along with a swiftness that was as deceptive as it was imperceptible.

In the matter of meat, his luck had been all in the beginning. The seven ptarmigan chicks and the baby weasel represented the sum of his killings. His desire to kill strengthened with the days, and he cherished hungry ambitions for the squirrel that chattered so volubly and always informed all wild creatures that the wolf-cub was approaching. But as birds flew in the air, squirrels could climb trees, and the cub could only try to crawl unobserved upon the squirrel when it was on the ground.

The cub entertained a great respect for his mother. She could get meat, and she never failed to bring him his share. Further, she was unafraid of things. It did not occur to him that this fearlessness was founded upon experience and knowledge. Its effect on him was that of an impression of power. His mother represented power; and as he grew older he felt this power in the sharper admonishment of her paw; while the reproving nudge of her nose gave place to the slash of her fangs. For this, likewise, he respected his

Chapter **5**

THE LAW OF MEAT

The cub's development was rapid. He rested for two days, and then ventured forth from the cave again. It was on this adventure that he found the young weasel whose mother he had helped eat, and he saw to it that the young weasel went the way of its mother. But on this trip he did not get lost. When he grew tired, he found his way back to the cave and slept. And every day thereafter found him out and ranging a wider area.

He began to get accurate measurement of his strength and his weakness, and to know when to be bold and when to be cautious. He found it expedient to be cautious all the time, except for the rare moments, when, assured of his own intrepidity, he abandoned himself to petty rages and lusts.

He was always a little demon of fury when he chanced upon a stray ptarmigan. Never did he fail to respond savagely to the chatter of the squirrel he had first met on the blasted pine. While the sight of a moose-bird almost invariably put him into the wildest of rages; for he never forgot the peck on the nose he had received from the first of that ilk he encountered.

A   B

Gestures also have low memorability. Especially when applications attach many different gestures to different possible actions, gesture interference and forgetting happens, and users have a hard time keeping track of what gesture goes with what action.

Clear for iPhone (**Figure 3.11**), a to-do list app, prides itself in eliminating the chrome. All the interaction in this interface is carried out through gestures. When the app is first started, a tutorial and an example list teach users how to use the app. The problem is that even users who patiently sit through the tutorial cannot remember the many gestures they are supposed to use for the actions. Although the example list gets them started, one of the first things users do is erase the items in this list, effectively removing much needed life lines that later on will be essential for using the app. Finally, even if users succeed in creating a list (a feat that few of our users accomplished), no tips or interface buttons remind them of what actions are available to them.

An app like Clear can work, but it needs to use tips more actively and to disclose information progressively in the right context rather than flooding users with it in the beginning.

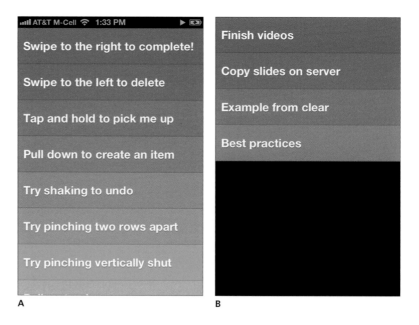

Figure 3.11 Clear for iPhone, a to-do list app, prides itself in eliminating the chrome. All the interaction in this interface is carried out through gestures. (**A**) The app starts with a tutorial and an example list. (**B**) Once users create a list, no tips or interface buttons remind them of what actions are available to them.

Gestures that have a tight metaphorical connection to the physical world tend to be the easiest to learn and remember, because they will be similar to gestures people have done in the past. Examples that have worked well are the page-turning gestures we just discussed, and the pinch-zoom gestures where you make something bigger by stretching it to expand its size and smaller by squeezing it. The more arbitrary the gesture, the harder it is to learn.

The best gestural learning is by doing, not by memorization. Apps can use multiple gestures to free screen space from the tyranny of chrome but must do so wisely by gently guiding the user via progressive disclosure and contextual tips, and by utilizing gesture-action pairs with the right affordances.

Chrome's benefits

Although expensive in screen space, chrome has considerable benefits:

- Chrome empowers users by providing a steady set of commands and options that are always visible (or at least easily revealed if our guidelines are followed). Chrome also stays in the same spot, liberating users from having to locate it. In addition, users are freed from the whims of particular Web page or content designers, which is one reason the Back button is one of the most popular features on the Web. Chrome might be overhead in terms of screen pixels, but it is power at the user's fingertips that serves as an immediate escape hatch from obnoxious or useless Web pages or apps.

Mobile Usability

- Chrome offers a set of generic commands that work on all the different types of content and data that appear within its framework. Because it's always the same, users have less to learn, meaning that they can focus on their real-world needs rather than on the computer.

- Chrome promotes consistency and standards in the user interface, which facilitate learnability and makes users feel even more in control of their experiences. (Of course, this applies only if you follow the standards rather than invent your own weird chrome to confuse users.)

On balance, chrome is good for usability. Just don't overdo it.

Overloaded vs. Generic Commands

One way to manage interaction design complexity and save screen space is to have commands serve double duty. There are two ways of doing this with different usability implications:

- Generic commands use the same command in different contexts to achieve conceptually the same outcome, even though details of the specific effects might differ.

- Overloaded commands use variants of the same command to achieve different outcomes—sometimes depending on the context and other times depending on where the command appears on the screen.

The most famous generic command these days is the pinch-zoom gesture, which works in most touch-screen UIs. In fact, the command is so pervasive that users expect it to work universally and are sorely disappointed when they encounter an application that doesn't support it. Pinching out sometimes enlarges text and other times enlarges pictures. Users don't know or care about the differences; they simply rely on the gesture as a generic command when they encounter content that's too small and want to make it bigger.

Generic commands increase usability, because they allow users to learn one thing and use it many times. Memories are strengthened by repeated activation, so the more places the command works, the better users will learn it.

Overloaded commands: Often confusing

You might think that overloaded commands are good as well. Having the same command achieve different (but similar) results sounds like an equally sound idea. In practice, however, command overloading often confuses users.

If a single command has different results depending on context, users often overlook the context and don't understand why they get different outcomes when doing the "same" thing.

When a single screen has multiple instances of what seems to be the same command, users often assume that the design is redundant and that all instances of the command will have the same effect. Or, when users simply grab onto the first instance they see, they often fail to notice that the command actually appears multiple times.

A classic example of overloaded commands is websites with multiple search fields. We can't count how many times we've seen users issue a query in the wrong search on such sites.

We saw several examples of confusing command overloading in our Kindle Fire user testing. For example, the *Condé Nast* magazine app has one Home button at the top of the screen that takes users to the list of magazines and another Home button that takes users to the Kindle home screen (**Figure 3.12**).

Figure 3.12 Two Home buttons in *Condé Nast's* Kindle Fire app.

These two buttons have different icons and appear in different locations, but they're still confusing.

For a decade, one of the primary homepage usability guidelines has been to designate a single page as the one-and-only official homepage for any given website. Users are confused when several pages are referred to as Home. In other words, don't use Home as an overloaded command within a website. The main page for a subsite should be called something else, such as "foobar main page," "foobar overview," or—if you must—"foobar home" (within the site's foobar section).

For mobile apps it's usually a good idea to have an "application home" that users can return to as a safe base after exploring the app's various areas. This is particularly important for content-rich apps, such as magazines or newspapers. Used this way, the Home button serves as a generic command: Conceptually it always does the same thing, even though the specific place users return to differs in different apps.

In contrast, offering many different "homes" within the same site or app makes Home an overloaded command, which is confusing.

Even worse, the Back button has many different interpretations. Thus:

- In many apps, Back means undo or "back to the previous screen" (which is the recommended use).

- In ESPN on Kindle Fire, Back means "up" in the information hierarchy, and most of the time it translates into "back to home screen" (and should thus be a Home button).

- In the *New York Times* on Kindle Fire, Back sometimes means "one step back" and sometimes means "two steps back." (When our users did a search and clicked through to an article, tapping Back didn't return them to the search listing, but rather bounced them back one step further.)

- In Zappos for Ice Cream Sandwich, Back on the homepage means backing out of the app regardless of whether the previous visited page was within the app; Back on a different page means undo (**Figure 3.13**).

So, if a Zappos user is on a product page (Figure 3.13A) and then accidentally taps the logo, the user would go to the homepage (Figure 3.13B). Unfortunately, tapping the virtual back button at this time takes the user out of the app rather than undoing the accidental move.

Figure 3.13 Zappos app for Android: (**A**) product page and (**B**) homepage. Back on the product page works as undo, but Back on the homepage takes the user out of the app.

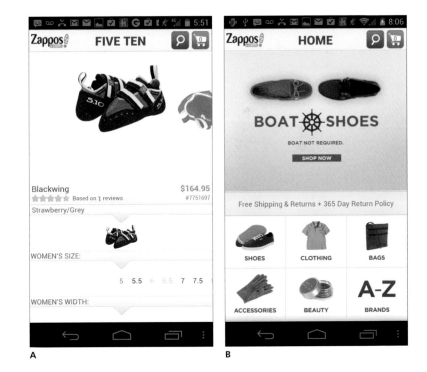

A   B

In its design guidelines for the latest Android version, Google made explicit the two meanings of Back that often cause confusion in many apps: Back as undo and Back as up (**Figure 3.14**).

Back as undo is usually used when users want to revert to the previous state because something went wrong. Back as up comes into play when people need to go up in the information hierarchy to a higher level. Most apps implement Back as up rather than Back as undo, causing trouble for their users.

Figure 3.14 The Ice Cream Sandwich version of the Google+ app. Ice Cream Sandwich distinguishes between the two different meanings of Back. In Ice Cream Sandwich, the virtual Back button at the bottom of the screen is supposed to mean undo, and the little caret (left-pointing arrow) at the top next to the icon is supposed to mean up to the previous level.

A final example of the risks from overloaded commands is the swipe ambiguity we found in our iPad user testing (see the section "Swipe Ambiguity" in Chapter 5). When the same command (a swipe gesture) has different outcomes, depending on exactly where and how the user swipes, confusion results unless the distinctions are clearer than they were in the apps we tested.

Effective command reuse

As the preceding examples show, it can be a bit tricky to determine whether command reuse should count as a generic command (usually good) or an overloaded command (usually bad). There are two key deciding factors:

- Do people recognize that two contexts are different? For example, two different websites are usually so different that users wouldn't expect the two sites' Home buttons to lead to identical destinations. In contrast, the context for two search boxes on the same screen is similar, even if the labels (which users rarely read) are different.

- Do people view the outcomes as similar or different? For example, returning to the previous screen is a strong enough concept that users will view Back commands as conceptually similar, even though the previously screens will usually differ.

Both criteria depend on how users interpret the user interface. How can you know what they'll think? Well, you could analyze it yourself and try to judge the strength of the similarities and differences. But empirical testing is safer.

Case Study: Optimizing a Screen for Mobile Use

During a lecture tour of Asia–Pacific, we took the opportunity to conduct several usability studies. One of the mobile sites we tested was AllKpop.com (**Figure 3.15**), which covers a topic of seemingly great fascination in many Asian countries: Korean pop stars.

Figure 3.15 AllKpop.com mobile site, as tested in Hong Kong.

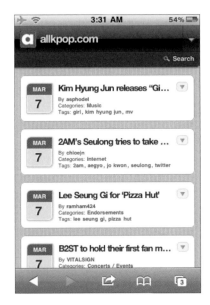

The AllKpop site does many things right:

- Most important of all, it supports a task that's perfect for mobile use: celebrity gossip. We've known since our first mobile usability studies in 2000 that killing time is a killer app for mobile. Many other tasks make little sense in the mobile scenario; no matter how great the design, the mobile versions wouldn't get much use and creating them is a waste of time.

- Almost as important, it has a separate mobile version, as we recommend in Chapter 2, "Mobile Strategy."

- Because the server auto-senses whether they're using a mobile or a desktop device, users don't have to manually choose their version. As we know from testing, usability drops dramatically when the mobile and full sites have different URLs because users often end up with the wrong user interface.

- Touch targets for each headline are fairly large.

- Content-carrying keywords usually appear at the beginning of the headlines. For this site, the pop star's name is the most important information for users, and it typically appears first.

However, the site doesn't follow all the guidelines for mobile usability, so we decided to create an alternative design that did (**Figure 3.16**).

Figure 3.16 Our proposed redesign of AllKpop's mobile homepage.

Our redesign included ten major changes:

1. **Fewer features**, which we achieved by removing three elements:

    - Bylines, because they aren't needed to choose an article (which is the only point of listing headlines on the front page)

    - Selectable categories and tags, which were too small to tap reliably anyway (and categories like Music seem worthless on a pop site)

    - The triangle button that displays a summary in place (instead, we always show a summary)

2. **Bigger touch targets** so the entire story tile can now be tapped, and users no longer need the added precision of tapping the actual headline. (In the live design, each tile contains several tiny tappable areas with low usability and questionable utility.)

3. **Full headlines** instead of truncated headlines. This is probably the biggest redesign improvement, because the full headline provides substantially stronger information scent (see the sidebar "Information Scent") than the few words visible on the live site. Truncating headlines or product names is never a good idea and sometimes can cause serious usability issues, as illustrated by the two examples in **Figure 3.17**. In both those cases, users need to take an extra step to understand what the headline is about (Figure 3.17A) or what the product might be (Figure 3.17B). Although users do scan when reading online, just the beginning of a text does not always offer sufficient information to disambiguate the content being read. This is especially true for product listings, where many products may start with the same string. In Figure 3.17b, 11 products start with the words "Blendtec" and eight of those have a similar picture.

4. **Enhanced scannability** by highlighting each pop star's name in the headlines.

5. **Even more information scent** by showing a short story summary (a "dek") under each headline.

6. **Using pop star photos** instead of date icons. Not only does this add some visual interest, but it further enhances scannability and information scent, as many users will recognize their favorite star's face faster than they can read a headline.

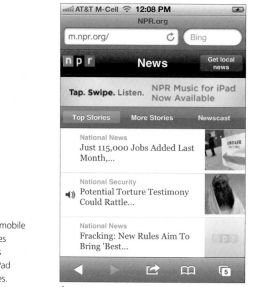

Figure 3.17 (A) NPR's mobile
site (m.npr.org) truncates
headlines. (B) Amazon's
Windowshop app for iPad
truncates product names.

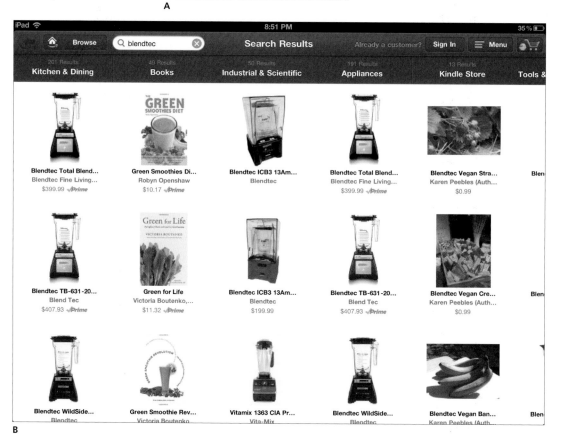

7. **Room for four full-story tiles** without scrolling. The slightly tighter spacing lets users view the entire fourth story summary in their first scan of the page. If users do scroll down, the ability to view more tiles in less space also means that they work less for each new story, so they're likely to want to see more of them. Because this second benefit is relatively small, we considered making the tiles smaller to display more stories on the first screen. On balance, the added information scent from the story summaries and pop star photos seemed a better use of the space, but testing an alternative would be worthwhile.

8. **Showing the publication date only as a divider** between stories published on different dates. The date of the last update is very important information on a news site, in general, and is essential on mobile: Because of connectivity issues, users might be looking at yesterday's news and not realize it. (**Figure 3.18** shows a good and a bad example of indicating dates in news apps.) However, because so many stories are published each day, users typically see only the current day's date when they access the site unless they scroll down far enough to reach yesterday's news. Thus the story date is not worth the substantial screen real estate it occupies in the live design. In general, it's good to *question any mobile design that repeats the same information* multiple times.

Figure 3.18 The date of the last update is essential for content that changes often. Two *New York Times* apps: (**A**) Android and (**B**) iPhone. The Android version does a better job of indicating when the articles were last updated. The iPhone app mentions only the time (but not the date) of the last update. Also, the time stamp is hidden by default (users must pull down the text to get to it).

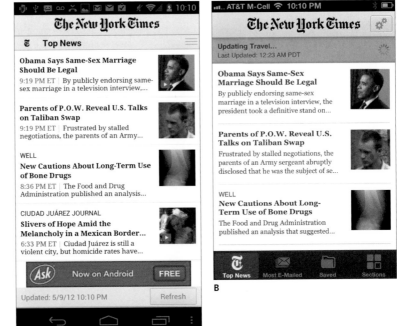

9. **Adding more space between the navigation bar's two options** so users are less likely to touch the wrong one.

10. **Labeling the drop-down menu** instead of simply denoting it by a triangle. (It's just above search in the original design—a subtle presentation that's mostly overlooked by users. In general, menus need to be signaled well so people can discover them; see **Figure 3.19**. And even when they are discoverable, in order for people to use them, they need to be labeled so users can easily guess what might be hidden under them.) Depending on which commands are actually in the menu, a different name might be better. We didn't redesign the entire navigation system, but we assumed that a revised categorization system would be the most valuable and usable way to navigate the site after headline tapping and search.

As this example shows, even a small mobile screen has room for many user interface intricacies. Even though this site (appropriately enough) has very few features, we made ten usability improvements—including cutting the features even more.

The tighter the design constraints, the more you must polish the user interface to deliver optimal usability. And mobile is an incredibly constrained design problem.

Figure 3.19 ESPN Score Center for Android: (**A**) The app uses a pull-up menu at the bottom of the screen. (**B**) The options inside the menu become visible when the pull-up menu is expanded. Unfortunately many of our users did not notice the little arrow at the bottom of the screen.

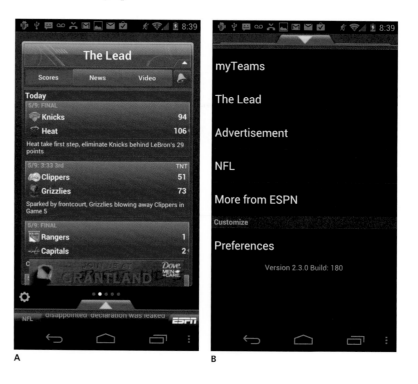

Mobile Usability

Information foraging is the most important concept to emerge from human-computer interaction research since 1993. Developed at the Palo Alto Research Center (previously Xerox PARC) by Stuart Card, Peter Pirolli, and colleagues, information foraging uses the analogy of wild animals gathering food to analyze how humans collect information online.

To say that Web users behave like wild beasts in the jungle sounds like a joke, but there's substantial data to support this claim. Animals make decisions on where, when, and how to eat on the basis of highly optimized formulas. Not that critters run mathematical computations, but rather that suboptimal behaviors result in starvation and thus fewer offspring that follow those behaviors in subsequent generations. After thousands of generations, optimal food-gathering behavior is all that's left.

Humans are under less evolutionary pressure to improve their Web use, but basic laziness is a human characteristic that might be survival related (don't exert yourself unless you have to). In any case, people like to get maximum benefit for minimum effort. That's what makes information foraging a useful tool for analyzing online media.

Information foraging's most famous concept is information scent: Users estimate a given hunt's likely success from the spoor, assessing whether its path exhibits cues related to the desired outcome. Informavores will keep clicking as long as they sense (to mix metaphors) that they're "getting warmer"—the scent must keep getting stronger and stronger or people give up. Progress must seem rapid enough to be worth the predicted effort required to reach the destination.

The most obvious design lesson from information scent is to ensure that links and category descriptions explicitly describe what users will find at the destination. Faced with several navigation options, it's best if users can clearly identify the trail to the prey and see that other trails are devoid of anything edible.

Therefore, don't use made-up words or your own slogans as navigation options, because they don't have the scent of the sought-after item. Plain language also works best for search engine visibility: Searching provides a literal match between the words in the user's mind and the words on your site.

Additionally, as users drill down the site, each page should clearly indicate that the users are still on the path to the food. In other words, provide feedback about the current location and how it relates to users' tasks.

Iterative design steps

Even the most talented genius designer can't design the perfect user interface in one attempt, and admittedly, neither can we. Instead, we used iterative design in our exercise to redesign the mobile AllKpop.com site (shown in Figure 3.15).

The biggest problem in iteration #1 (**Figure 3.20**) was using text from the beginning of each article for the summaries. Often these words didn't do the job of supplementing the headline to give users a preview of the article's main points. For iteration #2 we wrote custom summaries.

Figure 3.20 Redesign
iteration #1 for AllKpop.com.

Figure 3.21 Design iterations
of the SNSD group's thumbnail.

A second problem was the thumbnail for the first story about the
nine-member "Girls' Generation" group SNSD. It's tough to show
several people in 50x50 pixels. **Figure 3.21** shows some alternate
thumbnails we considered: In general, the closer you crop the photo,
the more recognizable the thumbnail.

For iteration #2 (**Figure 3.22**) we reintroduced two features from
the live site: the search and the publication date. It's good to remove
features, but these two were too important to miss.

Figure 3.22 Redesign
iteration #2.

Mobile Usability

We reintroduced some simplification by aggregating less-used navigation methods into a single drop-down menu. However, in iteration #2, the menu and search options were too small and close together for touch-screen use. We fixed this in iteration #3, which is shown in Figure 3.16.

Here we further enhanced headline scannability by highlighting the featured pop star's name.

Testing needed

Figure 3.16 shows our final redesign. However, this is not truly the "final" redesign. If we'd done this as a consulting project for a real client instead of as a simple exercise, the next step would have been user testing.

The redesign includes several questionable elements that would benefit from a usability study to be resolved:

- Would it be better to have smaller story tiles and show more stories on each screenful?

- Do people realize that the top date stripe is the publication date for all the stories between it and the next date stripe (which is usually one or two screenfuls below the fold)?

- Could headlines, deks, and thumbnails be written/cropped better? What do people look for when choosing articles to read? Content usability is usually the biggest determinant of website success:

  - In particular, what's the best way of depicting a group in a thumbnail? A close-up shot of a single singer (the last idea in the set of four SNSD attempts in Figure 3.21) seemed too focused on that individual. In our final design, we picked more of an "action" shot of one singer in costume to make it feel more like a performance than a portrait. But would it be better to show two or three singers?

  - Is it better to retain the same thumbnail at all times for any given star, or should we have a photo editor pick new pictures that better illustrate each story? New thumbnails are obviously more interesting, but persistent thumbnails promote faster recognition and save download time because most image files will be cached.

- Do the headlines look tappable? Given that they look like complete entries, will users know that they can click them to get to the corresponding articles?

- Does the Categories menu work? Should it have a different name and/or contain different menu items?

- Is the Search function discoverable enough? Should it be replaced with a search box, or should the word Search have better contrast?

- Is the darker nuance of red used to highlight group names helpful or confusing?

- When you use a name's plural or possessive form, such as "SNSD's" in the sample screen shot, is it better to highlight the entire construct (including the apostrophe and the "s") or just the main name? That is, should it be **SNSD's** or **SNSD**'s? The former might look better, but the latter might be more scannable. Answering this question would require an elaborate eyetracking study that's almost certainly not worth doing because the difference between the two designs is likely to be less than 1 percent. So for this decision, it's probably better to rely on the visual designer's judgment rather than testing; we have bigger fish to fry that'll probably gain anywhere from 10–100 percent.

- What did we overlook in testing the live site? All the preceding items in this list name some "known unknowns," but the "unknown unknowns" are often more important: Every time you test a new design, new issues arise. You can't assume that you have a complete picture of all user experience questions just because you tested one corner of the design space. If you don't get any unexpected findings from usability testing, you didn't run the study right.

Fortunately user testing can be fast and cheap, so it should be possible to continue with several more iterations and get an even better design that would make even more money for the site.

Typing on Mobile

Most users hate typing on mobile, and there is reason for that.

Typing with virtual keyboards (that are displayed on the touch screen) is challenging, partly because users must visually attend to the keyboard. Unlike with a physical keyboard, where the location of the keys is eventually learned and users don't necessarily look at the keyboard when typing, most users hunt-and-peck rather than touch-type on a virtual keyboard. Another difference between physical and virtual keyboards is the haptic feedback. On a touch screen, one of

Fitts' Law from Human-Computer Interaction says that the time to reach a target (using the mouse or the finger) is proportional to the size of the target and inversely proportional to the distance to the target. That is, bigger targets are reached faster; targets closer to the initial position of the finger or the mouse are also reached faster.

The proper size of touch targets is measured in centimeters (or in inches, because the recommended 1 cm size is the same as 0.4 inches). Various device makers provide human-interface guidelines with touch targets measured in pixels, which you can potentially use instead, although they tend to underestimate the required size. We provide our guideline in centimeters, because that's a physical measurement in the real world. The reason for the guideline is to match users' fingers, which are definitely physical objects in the real world.

the problems that users have is knowing whether the movement was precise enough: Did they tap the right key or touch nearby? Haptic feedback solves that problem and makes it possible for users to touch-type.

That being said, the most popular touch screen phones have no physical keyboard. The reasons that phone designers have moved away from physical keyboards on phones are twofold: More space can be allocated to the screen, and many apps and mobile websites are oriented toward content consumption and do not involve heavy typing. (In our testing, those users who had a sliding physical keyboard on their phone did not use it much and relied on the virtual keyboard for most tasks other than email.)

Although people certainly don't like to be forced to type on mobile, they do type if they need to. By far the most popular mobile activity is sending text messages: According to statistics from ComScore, in March 2012, 74 percent of mobile U.S. users sent text messages. The next most popular activity was taking pictures (60 percent), followed by email (41 percent). But typing an email or a text message is fairly different than filling a form: Abbreviations and even typos have little consequence in an email or text, whereas their costs in a form can be a lot more substantial. Just imagine sending the book that you just bought to the wrong address or transferring the wrong amount of money from one account to another! Text suggestions work well in free-form text, but can be catastrophic when you must fill in name and address information.

Because forms are a nuisance on mobile, we recommend that you:

- Help users as much as possible with filling in a form by:
  - Letting them use abbreviations, sensible defaults, or well chosen suggestions (based on user history), or allowing them to use the camera, GPS, or voice for input (**Figure 3.23**).
  - Computing information whenever possible. For instance, compute the state based on zip code in the United States. Don't ask users to enter the type of credit card and the card number; compute the type based on the number.
  - Supporting cut and paste. Not everybody will know how to do it, but it will be easier for those who do.
  - Prepopulating known values. If users are already logged in, don't make them enter their email and address when completing a purchase.

Figure 3.23 (Left) Hipmunk app for Android uses the current location (as captured by the phone GPS) and the current date as sensible defaults for its hotel search. (Of course, users should be allowed to use a different location as well, should they desire.)

Figure 3.24 (Right) Net-a-porter app for Android uses a long checkout form that requests unessential information.

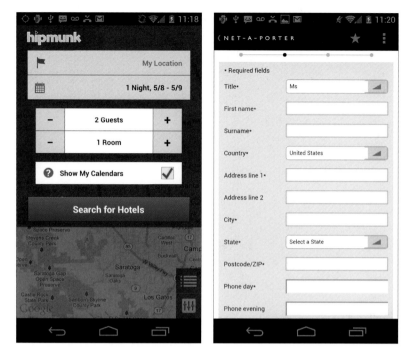

The target size recommendation comes from a paper published in 2006 in the Mobile HCI conference proceedings: P. Parhi, A.K. Karlson, and B.B. Bederson. "Target size study for one-handed thumb use on small touch screen devices." In Proceedings of the 8th Conference on Human-Computer Interaction with Mobile Devices and Services (Helsinki, Finland, September 12–15, 2006). MobileHCI '06, vol. 159. ACM, New York, NY, 203-210. DOI= http://doi.acm.org/ 10.1145/1152215. 1152260.

- Make the form as short as possible and ask for only essential information. Avoid asking users to type the same information twice. Forms like the one in **Figure 3.24** are daunting on mobile. Whenever possible, they should be reduced to require the essential information only. The title field, for instance, is not necessary: Even though it's a drop-down box and users don't actually need to type in that box, every extra field makes the form look more intimidating on mobile. Similarly, the evening phone (although optional) also makes the form look longer and more complex.

Even though typing is tedious, sometimes it is preferable to scrolling through screens and screens of information. For instance, it's easier for users to type the two-letter abbreviation of their state than to select a state from a 50-item drop-down box. It's also faster to start typing the name of a brand and pick among several matching suggestions than to find that brand in a list of thousands of brand names (**Figure 3.25**).

Although typing is particularly tricky on touch screens, tapping targets can also be difficult, especially if those targets are small. Research indicates that the ideal target size for touch is 1 cm by 1 cm. Usually width matters a bit more than height, but targets that are tiny and crowded pose a challenge for users. Not only do they take longer to reach those targets, but users are also more likely to make a mistake (**Figure 3.26**).

Figure 3.25 (Left) Zappos app for Android. When Zappos users want to filter their search result by brand, they must scroll through the many options available to get to the desired brand.

Figure 3.26 (Right) *USA Today* for Android. *USA Today* targets are far smaller than the ideal size of 1 cm by 1 cm for touch: The Subsection menu is very short, and the targets in the top navigation bar (News, Money, Sports, etc.) are too tiny and close to each other.

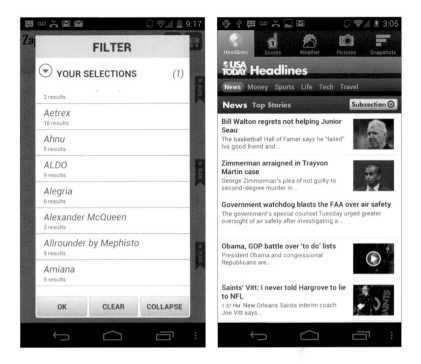

Download Times

One of the reasons that users perform poorly on mobile devices is speed. Even people with superfast smartphones are bound to encounter situations where their device is just too slow. This can be because the cellular network is too crowded, or because network coverage is poor in a given location. Wireless networks are still far from being ubiquitous, and especially when they're on the go, users rely on a cellular network signal to access the Internet on their mobile phone.

When speed is slow, every page load matters. Every page load is one more chance for a dropped connection. Most users don't have the patience to wait for a long time. If they are truly motivated to get to the information on your site, they may call a friend who's sitting at a computer and ask him or her to find that information for them. Or they may simply call your company, if they can find your number. Most often, however, they will just quit your site or application and go elsewhere.

Interaction Cost

Interaction cost refers to the number of atomic actions (for example, clicks, scrolls, switching attention to new windows) that a person needs to perform to fulfill a task on a computer, a mobile device, or a similar device. Every additional action users have to do is painful—or at least annoying.

Because speed is so important on mobile devices, usability issues are amplified. What's one extra click on the desktop? Although it is certainly not good usability practice to make your users do more work than necessary, your site will probably survive. Users will not be that bothered by an extra click when they are using a PC. However this is not true for a mobile device, where clicks (or taps) may translate into long download times. Users will not forgive you if your site or application makes them work too hard or wait too long. Hence, when designing for mobile devices, it is crucial to minimize interaction cost.

How do you get around slow speed?

- **Streamline the interaction** so it involves as few page downloads as possible. Sometimes "page downloads" may equal "taps," but not all taps lead to a page download. (For instance, if the content is stored locally on the phone, a tap in an app may not download any information from the server.)

  Figure 3.27 shows an example of unnecessary page loads from Zappos' mobile website. The site is too eager to compute the search refinements: If a user wants to look at men's black shoes, he cannot submit all three filter values ("shoes," "men," "black") at once. Instead, he needs to submit them separately, because once the user has selected the product type ("Shoes"), the site will automatically load the results without allowing him to fill in the other filter values.

- **Include only needed information** that is likely useful to your users and adds value to the page.

- **Don't abuse images** on a page. Many images usually equate to slow download times. That doesn't mean that you should not use images. In fact, users love beautiful pictures on their phones. It just means that you should choose your images wisely and not include a lot of them on a page.

- **Give users feedback** about the state of the download by showing them a progress bar. It won't prevent them completely from moving on if the site is too slow, but it may delay them just a bit.

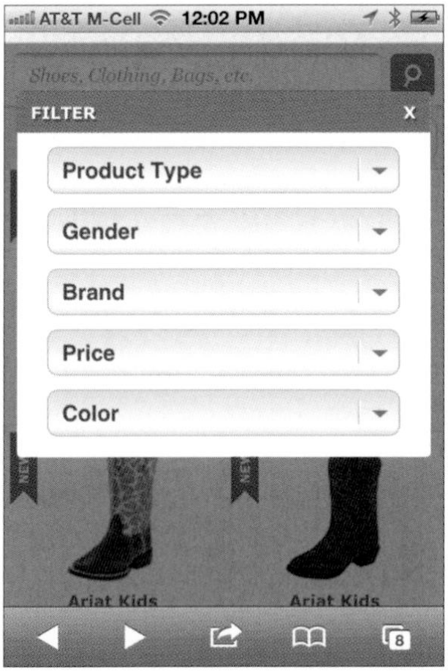

Figure 3.27 Zappos' mobile website (m.zappos.com) submits filter values one by one and inefficiently generates a page load for each of them.

Early Registration Must Die

One of the most important guidelines for mobile apps is to avoid making users pass through a registration screen as the first step.

In our testing we saw countless apps that asked users to register before the apps had proven their worth in the slightest. This is wrong. Remember that users start out with a fairly low level of commitment to your app. Unless yours is a truly great app that offers immense value, people won't use it enough to make registration worth their while.

Registration can certainly provide added business value and added usage convenience to your customers. But this is true only if people actually complete the registration. Unfortunately if you force users to register before they're sufficiently convinced of your app's value, many will simply back right out of the app and never try it again. You've then lost the one chance you'll ever get at making a first impression (actually, *any* impression).

Cautioning against early registration is hardly new. Since 1999 a key usability guideline for e-commerce shopping carts and checkout processes has been to allow users to buy without having to register. Sites that allow "guest checkout" have much higher conversion rates than sites that require users to make up a user ID and password before they're permitted the rare privilege of forking over their money. After all, we can't allow just *anybody* to shop at our site—or at least that seems to be the thinking.

Registration will also cost you business on desktop websites where it's only somewhat of a pain. In the mobile environment, every extra hoop that users must jump through causes considerably more pain. In addition, users are less committed to an app they've just downloaded than they are to an e-commerce site where they've spent time browsing and adding items to a shopping cart.

When you combine more pain and less commitment, it's easy to see why upfront registration costs you even more lost business on mobile than on the desktop.

Although overall user experience is paramount, you must also pay attention to the details. A single bad screen can cost millions of dollars in lost revenue and brand value.

As the saying goes, you get only one chance to make a first impression. That's why startup screens are crucial. This is particularly true for mobile users, who often have fairly low motivation to mess with apps they've downloaded for free. But even in "regular" software, the installation, setup, and initial screens can make or break an app.

Figure 3.28 shows two apps that both require users to sign up, but they take completely different approaches. Zapd, an app for posting content to the Web, lets people use the app and asks them to sign up only when they want to actually post the content they have created.

Figure 3.28 (**A**) Zapd for iPhone allows users to create content and requires them to sign up only when they want to post that content to the Web. (**B**) Orchestra for iPhone requires users to sign up upfront before actually using the app.

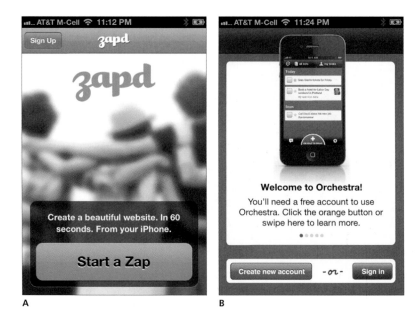

A   B

Orchestra, a to-do list app, doesn't give any access to the app before creating an account; it doesn't even tell users what the app is going to do. Why would a to-do list app even require an account? Orchestra probably wants to sync its lists on multiple platforms; however, a better experience would allow people to use the app and request that they sign up only if they care about list synchronization.

Registration on the first screen is an example of "take before you give": Apps want users to spend time and effort without any perceived benefit. Asking for permission to send notifications or use the current location before users find out what the app is about (**Figure 3.29**) is another way in which apps abuse their emerging relationship with the users. Often users have no idea of the purpose of these actions (use of current location and sending notifications).

Figure 3.29 (**A**) Amici's, a pizza chain, asks permission to send push notifications when the app is first launched. (**B**) Wolfram Alpha for iPad, a mathematical search engine, asks permission to use the current location when the app is first launched.

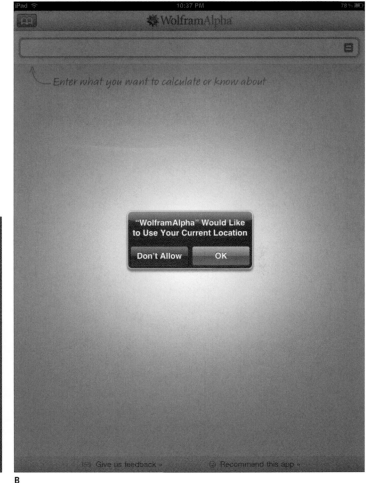

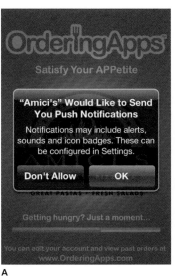

A

B

Another example of "take before you give" is when apps start by presenting users with lengthy instructions or user manuals (**Figure 3.30**). Most users are not motivated to read the instructions before getting any value from the app. And user manuals and tutorials don't work, even when users are forced to sit through them, mostly because they are out of context and people won't be able to memorize all the information anyway. If you must do it, take the quick, top-of-the-interface route exemplified by Foodspotting (Figure 3.30A) rather than the lengthy and more arduous one taken by Marvel Comics (Figure 3.30B).

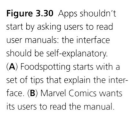

Figure 3.30 Apps shouldn't start by asking users to read user manuals: the interface should be self-explanatory. (**A**) Foodspotting starts with a set of tips that explain the interface. (**B**) Marvel Comics wants its users to read the manual.

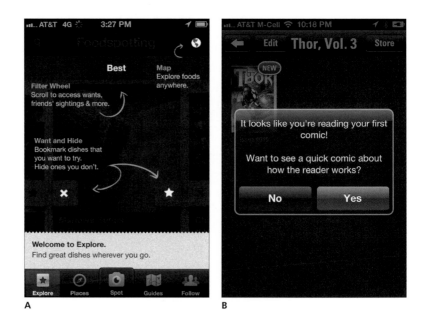

The initial experience should engage users and draw them in rather than make demands on them. At the first launch, the app has not proven its value to users and has not gained their trust. Our recommendations are 1) never ask for permission when the app is first launched (unless the app absolutely cannot work without that permission); 2) when you ask for such permission, always explain to the users why you need the current location and what the content of the notifications will be; and 3) avoid making users read long instructions or user manuals.

Example: Pizza Ordering Application

We saw many examples of too-early registration and too-burdensome screens in our various apps studies.

When the Pizza Hut app first launched on the iPhone, users were hit with the registration demand in **Figure 3.31** when all they wanted was to browse a selection of yummy pizzas. This was very off-putting to our test users.

What should the proper sequence be?

1. Show the list of basic pizzas.

2. Let users customize their order.

3. Show the price, along with any salient ordering info (perhaps after having users enter their zip code to get delivery times and such).

4. Take the order. At this point, it's appropriate to ask for personal info because users are now sufficiently committed.

To test the actual application, we forced users to proceed beyond this registration screen; in real use outside the lab, they would never have gone far enough to see a pizza.

Inside the app there were some smaller interaction design problems, but the company could still have doubled mobile pizza orders by getting rid of the upfront registration screen and asking users for their info *after* they had whetted their taste buds by showing them the pizzas.

None of the users clicked the button labeled "Not ready to order? Demo the app" in Figure 3.31. When we tried this button (for the sake of the experiment), Pizza Hut served up the exact user experience recommended in the preceding steps 1–4. So the designers knew how to do it, just not in the main UI flow.

Why didn't users try the demo feature? Because they didn't want a demo. They wanted to *see the pizzas* on offer. Although "just looking" is a classic shopping strategy, people don't tell a department store clerk that they're not quite ready to buy a new sweater, but they would like one demo'd. No; they enter the store, look at the sweaters (all lined up for that exact purpose), and try on the ones that most appeal to them. Only from the store's perspective would this scenario be considered "a demo." From the customer's perspective, it's simply "shopping," and you don't have to apply in triplicate for a permit to do so.

Although we've said it a million times, we apparently have to say it again: Speak the user's language in the UI.

Since we first tested this app, Pizza Hut has changed its design (**Figure 3.32**). The company no longer requires registration upfront but is still far from eliminating the starting hurdles. In the newer design, before users get to see the product selection and decide if they are interested, they have to think of whether they will want delivery or carryout, and in either case, they must specify an address: the delivery address or the place where they'll be picking up. That's a lot of work that users have to do with no reward in sight: Most people need a carrot (or a pizza) dangled in front of them before putting all that effort into an app.

Mobile apps obviously use a type of user interface, so it should come as no surprise that general UI guidelines apply in addition to the special mobile guidelines. The difference between mobile apps and desktop apps is that with the former, the UI guidelines are much more critical because mobile typically implies intermittent use. Thus the initial hurdles must be very low and easy to jump, or users will never get accustomed to using your app.

Case Study: The WSJ Mobile App

The *Wall Street Journal*'s iPhone app had just two stars in Apple's App Store in 2011. Averaged across 68,418 consumer reviews, the rating was not just a reflection of a few irate users.

As a rough estimate, a two-star average across 68,418 reviews means that 40,000 users gave the application a one-star rating. Given the 90-9-1 rule for social design, most users never bother reviewing products, so 40,000 low scores represent at least half a million dissatisfied customers.

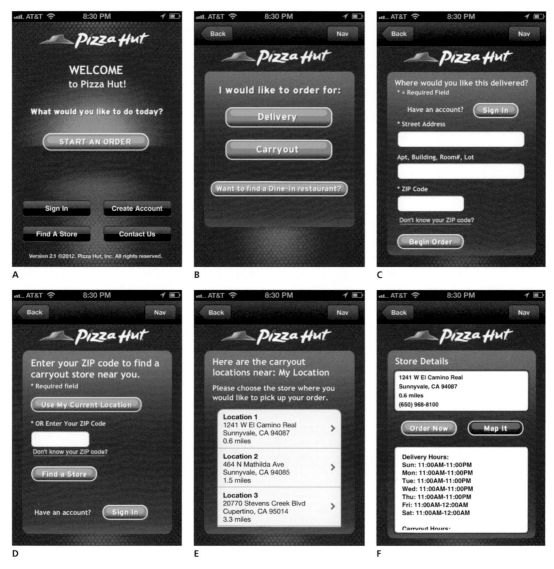

Figure 3.32 The newer version of Pizza Hut app for iPhone makes users go through several input-intensive steps before seeing any products: (**A**) Homepage; (**B**) Pressing "Start an order" on the homepage leads to a screen where users must decide if they want carryout or delivery. (**C**) If users select delivery, on the next screen they need to enter the delivery address. (**D**)–(**E**) If users select carryout, they must go through three different screens to find a carryout store near them. (**F**) After specifying either a carryout store or a delivery address, users can see the available menu.

The *WSJ* is one of the world's most respected newspapers and has long been a digital pioneer. How could it produce a two-star mobile app?

The answer was clear from reading the reviews. The three highest-rated reviews all gave one-star ratings, and their headings were:

- *"Slap."* (The first sentence? *"These guys have the nerve to charge additional fees to current online subscribers."*)
- *"Useless app, have to pay twice for same content."*
- *"Charging for content—twice!?!"*

It was clear that people were deeply offended by being asked to pay again for mobile access to the newspaper when they were already paying for a wsj.com subscription.

We would agree with these users if in fact they were being charged twice for the same articles. *But they were not.* Mobile app access was free to paying website subscribers: They simply had to log in with their existing user ID and password.

Confusing Startup Screen

Why did so many people think they had to pay for the WSJ iPhone app when they didn't? A highly confusing user interface design was the culprit. The first time you launched the app, the startup screen in **Figure 3.33** appeared.

The strongest call to action—in terms of placement and size—was the offer to subscribe and get two weeks free. (Implying, of course, that there would be a fee after this period.) Pressing the Subscribe Now button displayed the screen in **Figure 3.34**.

Figure 3.33 (Left) The WSJ iPhone app in 2011: Startup screen.

Figure 3.34 (Right) The WSJ iPhone app: The screen shown after tapping Subscribe Now.

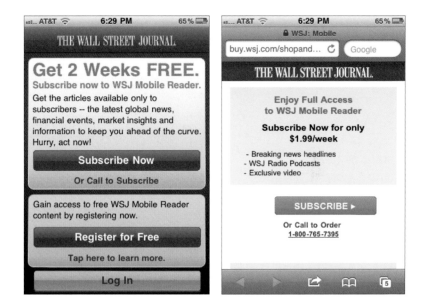

It was obvious that it would cost $1.99 per week to use the mobile app after the first two weeks. Although this was the only logical conclusion, *it was false*. If you clicked the Subscribe button on the second screen, you'd see a screen saying that access was free for current website subscribers.

However most users never saw this third screen. The Subscribe button had zero information scent for current subscribers. Past experience from all websites and apps uniformly led people to the same conclusion: Subscribe was the call to action for establishing a *new* subscription. Thus, as soon as users saw the second screen, they backed out if they didn't want to pay twice for the same articles.

Most people probably gave up at that point, because using the app so clearly seemed to cost an extra $1.99 per week. If some users were particularly persistent, however, they might have returned to the startup screen and tried the second button, Register for Free.

The second button led to a registration screen where you could create a new account that gave free access to a small number of articles. You weren't told that you could use your existing website account if you had one. Again, the only sensible conclusion was that you could access the full set of articles only by ponying up again and paying the extra $1.99 per week.

Wildly persistent users might have noticed the much smaller Log In area at the bottom of the startup screen. However they were unlikely to press this button because their experience with the app so far had taught them that they needed to register (and pay extra) before being allowed to log in.

Those few users who pressed Log In finally saw that they could use their existing wsj.com credentials to access the app. However, as the many negative App Store reviews attested, few users ever made it this far.

(Also, our tests of hundreds of mobile apps and websites have clearly shown a strong user preference for engaging with the top option. Even though phone screens are small, users might still overlook the last option, as they focus their attention on the top of the screen.)

Degrading the Brand

Does it matter that existing website subscribers give up on the mobile app? After all, the company *already has its money* from the website subscription.

Also, the design works reasonably well for new subscribers who are the only ones generating incremental revenue. So why not just focus on new subscribers and ignore old customers and their horrible user experience?

Well, there are two reasons not to disregard existing customers:

- Existing subscribers feel so insulted by having to pay twice that their negative ratings dominate the App Store feedback. Thus many potential new subscribers will see the two-star rating and immediately abandon the application download. With 500,000 alternatives, people don't have time for junk apps.

- People who've paid for website access are the newspaper's most loyal fans. Paying for Web content is fairly rare; customers willing to do so should be treasured, not treated like garbage.

Newspapers have two strategic imperatives for surviving in the Internet age:

- **Retain credibility** with their users. They must be more highly respected than the random sites users dredge up on Google.

- **Deepen relationships** with loyal users, so they turn to the paper first instead of using one of the many aggregators that commoditize content.

Credibility and relationships take a dive when customers are mistreated, particularly when they feel *unfairly* wronged.

The long-term impact of the *WSJ* confusing application UI is a severe erosion of the *WSJ* brand among the people who matter most: loyal, paying readers. As this case perfectly exemplifies, usability is not just a matter of whether users can press the correct button. User experience is branding in the interactive world.

Another difficulty stems from the newspaper's convoluted subscription model: Print subscribers must pay extra to access the online version. This requires an extra layer of explanation to distinguish different kinds of subscribers. For the sake of the redesign shown in the next section, "A Better Design," we're not touching the pricing model, but it does complicate the UI and thus reduces the conversion rate.

A second reason to give print subscribers free access is obvious. They're the most valuable customers: Print advertising is more effective than online advertising because broadsheet layouts have a stronger impact. Thus a newspaper should encourage readers to maintain their print subscriptions by treating them well. However it's beyond the scope of this section to resolve the trade-off between making short-term money by overcharging print subscribers versus the long-term loss of pushing people away from print.

A Better Design

If a bad screen can cost millions, a better screen is worth a lot. **Figure 3.35** shows our idea for an alternative startup screen for the *WSJ* app.

Figure 3.35 Our proposed redesign of the WSJ startup screen.

This screen eliminates the horrible usability problem discussed earlier by making it clear that existing subscribers can use their existing account to access the app. Also:

- It's clear that there are three possible scenarios, because the use cases are spelled out rather than implied.

- Placing buttons side by side and below the form reduces the possibility that users will overlook one and simply choose the first option. (**Figure 3.36** and **Figure 3.37** show why other placements are not good enough.)

- A simplified workflow eliminates the ambiguity between subscribing and registering, and presents fewer options on the first page.

We also changed how the price for new subscribers was presented—$103.48 per year instead of $1.99 per week—because the customer's credit card is charged the full annual fee at sign up. Being dinged for $103 when you expect a $2 charge is a highly negative experience and probably the source of many customer-service calls.

The second screen can put greater emphasis on enticing new users to pay for full rather than limited access. For example, the screen could state that the subscription fee equates to only $1.99 per week or 33¢ per day (*WSJ* publishes only six editions per week). Here it would be prudent to run an A/B test comparing annual versus weekly cost information on the first screen.

Figure 3.36 (Left) Snapguide app for iPhone. Another popular login pattern is to have two tabs for the sign-in and register options at the top of the screen. Most users don't notice the two tabs and start typing right away, whether or not they have an account.

Figure 3.37 (Right) Orchestra app for iPhone. Forms that have the main Submit (or, in this case, Sign Up) button at the top of the screen do not work well, because they go against the normal workflow: When users finish filling in the form, they typically tap the button underneath without paying attention to the top of the screen.

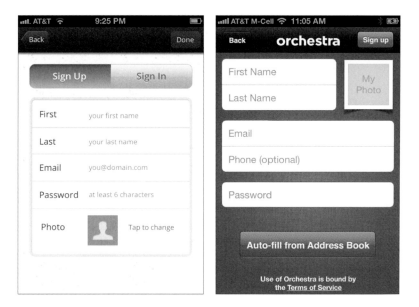

That said, you should change to a weekly price only if it offers dramatically better conversion. If weekly prices are only slightly better, it's best to show the annual price rather than suffer the long-term penalties of reducing brand reputation by subjecting customers to a bait-and-switch tactic.

One of A/B testing's main weaknesses is that it encourages an overly short-term focus on users' initial behavior. It's easy to overlook the long-term effect of design changes if you look only at clicks, which is one reason we like supplementing A/B tests with qualitative tests that give more insight into users' thinking.

Initially we were tempted to remove the Call to Subscribe link from the startup screen. (Phone contact info should definitely be on the "detailed info" screen.) Our guess is that the *WSJ* gets numerous customer-service calls because of the current confusing design. Once we make access for existing subscribers obvious and remove the misleading pricing for new subscribers, calls should drop to a fraction of the existing volume. (The near elimination of customer-support costs is one of the key ROI metrics for usability.)

However we kept the call-in number in this redesign for two reasons:

- Our testing shows that being willing to disclose your phone number is a strong credibility marker that enhances a design's persuasive value.

- There could be other issues—such as expired passwords or declined credit cards—that drive call volume. The company's own call center stats will show this, but we don't have the data. Also, our studies of the mobile user experience show that many people are reluctant to enter credit card numbers on their smartphones, which aren't seen as being as safe as a wired connection. This might change, but currently it's best for m-commerce to offer an alternate payment channel.

A New WSJ Workflow

The initial *WSJ* app experience involved two distinct choices:

- New versus existing subscribers
- Paid full access versus free limited access

It's possible to bundle all of this into a single screen (as shown in **Figure 3.38**), but the resulting UI would be too complex and error prone for mobile use.

Instead we decided on a two-step workflow: First, you branch between new and old users; second, two different screens handle each case with an appropriate design for the specific circumstances.

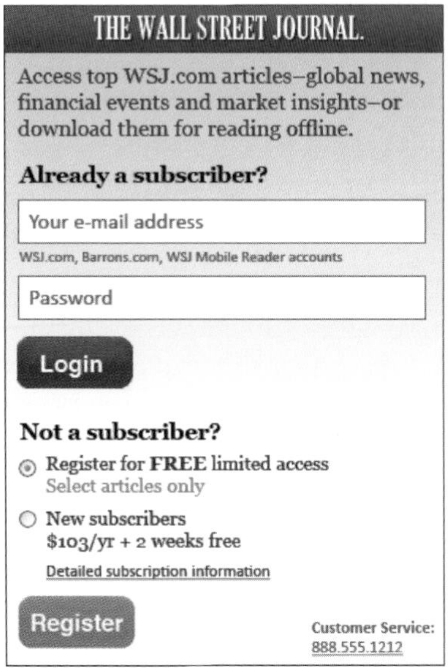

Figure 3.38 An alternative launch screen with a fast-track option for registered users. (This design is not recommended, because the design is error prone for new users.)

THE WALL STREET JOURNAL.

Access top WSJ.com articles–global news, financial events and market insights–or download them for reading offline.

Already a subscriber?

Your e-mail address

WSJ.com, Barrons.com, WSJ Mobile Reader accounts

Password

Login

Not a subscriber?

- Register for **FREE** limited access
  Select articles only
- New subscribers
  $103/yr + 2 weeks free
  Detailed subscription information

Register

Customer Service:
888.555.1212

The two-step workflow's obvious penalty is that users must pass through the second screen each time they log in. However, because this is a low-security app, it should be possible to store the login credentials on the phone and log in users automatically upon subsequent uses. (A high-security app, such as online banking, couldn't do this, but it's no big loss if someone can read your newspaper for free after stealing your phone.)

Figure 3.38 shows an alternate workflow design that would allow existing subscribers to bypass the second screen by logging in directly from the first screen. We discarded this approach because it would cause too many usability problems for new users. In countless test sessions, we've seen users being seduced by the magnetism of open type-in fields. Users' action bias is so strong that many go straight where they can "do stuff" instead of reading the text or considering the totality of the options on the screen.

Ideally the next step is to user-test the redesign. You can do this with paper prototyping, so you don't have to fully implement a new app to see whether the new design solves the current design's usability problems.

Testing typically uncovers additional opportunities for improvement and thus produces an even better design. In this case, fielding a redesign of these few initial screens should allow the *Journal* to improve its App Store rating in short order. It would thus quickly pay for itself through increased downloads and account activations. The main payback, however, would come from the long-term benefit of no longer infuriating the company's most loyal customers.

Better Next Year

After we produced the redesign proposal discussed in the previous section, the *Wall Street Journal* released its own redesign in 2012. The new app is even better than our proposal, because the newspaper also changed the business model for the app—something we had not attempted when trying to simply design some new screens.

This is an old lesson, but it bears repeating: The true way to great user experience doesn't just come from great UI design. Total user experience encompasses everything the user meets, and the way you run the business is a big part of this. Often the business model can have greater impact on user experience than anything designers can do if they're not allowed to alter the business model.

Workflow design is a big issue in application usability. The wrong workflow can easily confuse the users, or force them into making errors or losing their work.

Figure 3.39 shows a flawed workflow for posting a picture to the Web in Zapd. Once users select their picture, they can adjust it, but if they don't like the result, they need to go back and choose another picture instead of being allowed to modify the original picture again. The workflow should allow users to inspect the result of their editing and make changes.

In many cases a tighter workflow best expedites the paths users take to their goals. But in many other cases it's better to add a few steps to ensure that each step is focused and self-explanatory. What matters to usability is not the number of clicks, but the amount of user frustration and time spent. For an app, there's no delay in moving from one screen to the next, so it's often better to resolve the trade-off in favor of additional screens. In contrast, as discussed earlier in the section "Download Times," mobile sites must be more conservative in adding steps because of the higher

Figure 3.39 Zapd for iPhone. The workflow for posting a picture is flawed: (**A**) First, users can tap the Photo button at the bottom of the screen; (**B**) second, they can take a picture or select one from their library; (**C**) third, they can move and scale the picture. (**D**) The next screen shows the result of the previous move/scale operation. If users are unhappy with the result and press the Cancel button, they must take a new picture or find the old one in the library again.

interaction cost imposed by the (currently slow) download delay for each added screen. **Figure 3.40** compares the checkout process in three different contexts. Walmart (Figure 3.40A–C) asks users to enter a shipping method, shipping address, and billing address on separate screens. An extra fourth screen reviews the order and allows users to place it. Contrast it with Nordstrom (Figure 3.40D), which compresses the process into only two steps: one for entering the billing and shipping info, and another for payment and review. On the Web, the fewer number of steps to complete a form, the better.

Workflow Design (continued)

At any point during the process, the user can get interrupted, and extra pages often mean extra wait times. In contrast, an app such as Zappos (Figure 3.40E), where the user is sent to separate screens to enter a shipping address and select a shipping method, can afford to split the checkout process into multiple screens, provided that the transition among them is instantaneous and that the app saves state (that is, if users get interrupted, the information they already entered would be preserved in the app).

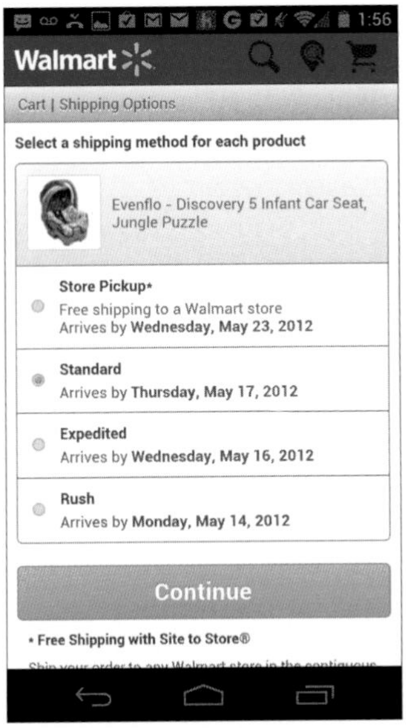

A

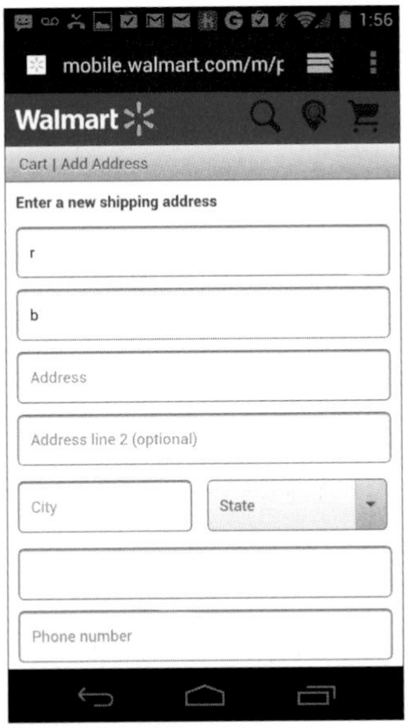

B

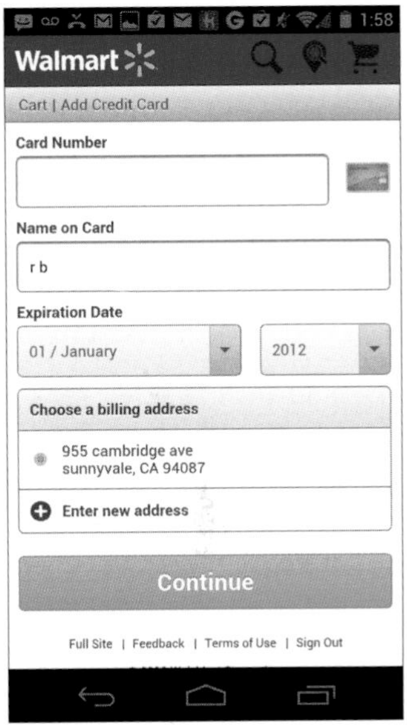

C

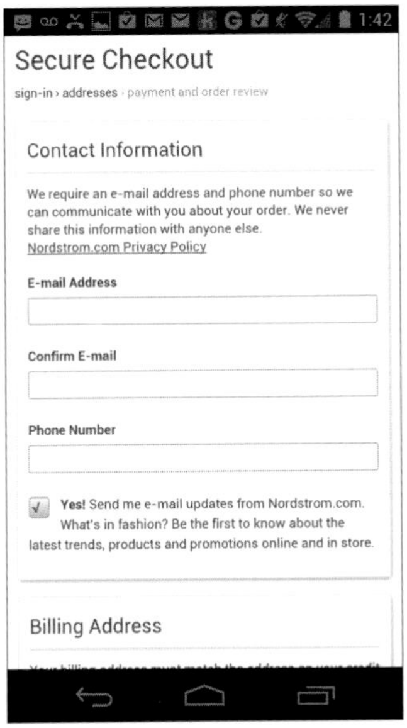

D

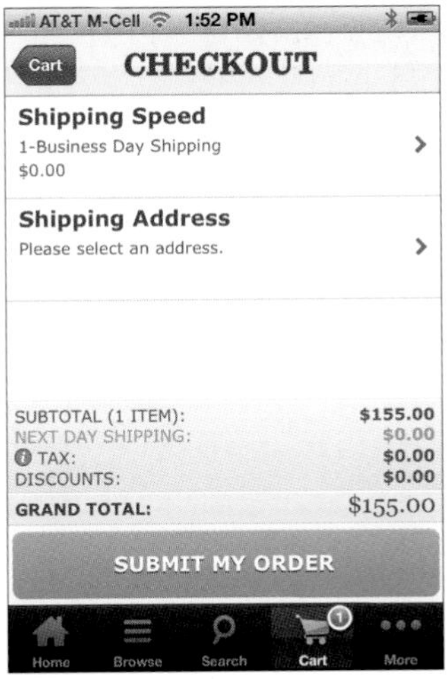

E

Figure 3.40 Steps for checking out: (**A**)–(**C**) Walmart's mobile site (m.walmart.com); (**D**) Nordstrom's mobile site (m.nordstrom.com); (**E**) Zappos app for iPhone.

Figure 3.41 shows the three steps a user would face the first time after downloading the new *WSJ* app. The very first screen shows some actual news, confirming that it is a newspaper app. It's much better to dump people right into the useful parts of the application instead of slapping them with an up-front registration demand before they can see whether the app is any good at all.

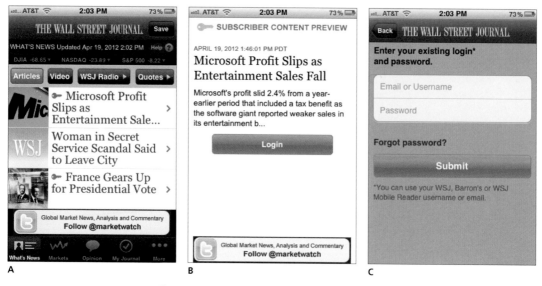

Figure 3.41 (**A**)–(**C**) Revised workflow on the *WSJ* iPhone app in 2012: The problem was fixed after a year of misery.

The first screen uses a key-shaped icon to denote "locked" articles that are available only to paying subscribers. Note that some articles are free to everybody. In the new app, users don't have to register to read the free articles. This allows one-click access to real content (not shown here), adding further immediate value. After reading a few free articles, users will hopefully be convinced that this app features genuine *WSJ* content, and they'll know whether or not they want to become paid users.

If the user clicks a locked story, the second screen appears with a short summary of the article and a big button to log in. The summary helps users decide whether this is really something worth the extra work of logging in. Many apps are too arrogant to help users decide, but it usually backfires to assume that everybody will want your information bad enough to jump through additional hoops without knowing more about what's on the other side of the fence.

In addition, a user who does want to log in will get the third screen, which makes it very clear how to use an existing account. It's less clear what to do if you don't have an account, but presumably you have to go to the website and pay there.

The new workflow is optimized for two classes of users: people with existing paid accounts and freeloaders who don't want to pay but want to see how much they can get for free. The design is less usable for people who are willing to pay but are not existing subscribers. Is this good? We can't say without knowing how many people are in each category. But it sounds credible that the *Wall Street Journal* would mainly get paid subscribers from people who either get the printed newspaper or who register on the website while they're in the office. So most likely this new design works very well for the company.

For sure, users like the new design. The new app got three-and-a-half stars in Apple's App Store, which is a huge step up from the miserable two stars collected by the old design.

The main reason the ratings aren't even higher is that some users don't like the ads—one more example of the business model impacting the user experience and thus the store ratings.

4 Writing for Mobile

We've run many user studies, watching people read information on mobile devices. Our research included mobile websites, apps, and email newsletters. Across all formats, there's one indispensable element: *focus*.

Of course, there are many other points to consider, but this one issue is the main usability guideline for mobile content: *When you're writing for mobile users, focus their attention on the essential content.*

As discussed in the next section, research has shown that it's 108 percent harder to understand information when reading from a mobile screen. Content comprehension suffers when you're looking through a peephole, because there's little visible context. The less you can see, the more you have to remember, and human short-term memory is notoriously weak.

Mobile Content Is Twice as Difficult

Research by R.I. Singh and colleagues from the University of Alberta shows that it's much harder to understand complicated information when you're reading through a peephole.

For full details of the research study discussed in this section, please see R.I. Singh, M. Sumeeth, and J. Miller: "Evaluating the Readability of Privacy Policies in Mobile Environments," International Journal of Mobile Human Computer Interaction, vol. 3, no. 1 (January–March 2011), pp. 55–78.

Singh and colleagues ran a Cloze test on the privacy policies of ten popular websites: eBay, Facebook, Google, Microsoft, Myspace, Orkut, Wikipedia, WindowsLive, Yahoo!, and YouTube.

We did a quick analysis of Facebook's privacy policy, which features:

- 5,789 words, or 35 times the number of words users read during an average page visit.

- 13th-grade reading level, so only people with a year or more of university would find the text easy to read.

- Nicely formatted for Web reading, including a good use of subheads, bulleted lists, and highlighted keywords in keeping with guidelines for writing for the Web. (That said, these guidelines also call for short text and an 8th-grade reading level when targeting a broad consumer audience, not just Harvard students.)

In any case, there's no doubt that privacy policies count as complicated Web content.

In Singh's study, 50 test participants completed Cloze tests while reading the privacy policies on either a desktop-sized screen or an iPhone-sized screen.

The study didn't use an actual iPhone, but because users didn't perform navigation or any interactions other than reading and scrolling, the specific device shouldn't impact the comprehension results.

Here are the results:

- **Desktop screen.** 39.18 percent comprehension score
- **Mobile screen.** 18.93 percent comprehension score

Test scores must be 60 percent or higher for text to be considered easy to understand. Even while reading from a desktop screen, users achieved only two-thirds of the desired comprehension level, showing that privacy policies do tend to be overly complicated.

The Cloze test is a common empirical comprehension test. It works as follows:

1. Replace every *N*th word in the text with blanks. A typical test uses *N* = 6, but you can make the test easier by using a higher *N* value.
2. Ask your test participants to read the modified text and fill in the blanks with their best guesses as to the missing words. Each person should work alone.
3. The score is the percentage of correctly guessed words. Because you're testing comprehension rather than spelling skills, synonyms and misspellings are allowed.

If users get 60 percent or more right on average, you can assume the text is reasonably comprehensible for the specified user profile employed to recruit test participants. There's a clear difference between readability scores and comprehension scores:

- Readability is a property of the actual text and predicts the education level typically needed for people to read the content without undue difficulty.
- Comprehension is a combined property of the text and a specific user segment, and indicates whether this target audience actually understands the material's meaning.

Here's an example using a paragraph from Facebook's privacy policy:

Site activity information. We keep {1}_____ of some of the actions {2}_____ take on Facebook, such as {3}_____ connections (including joining a group {4}_____ adding a friend), creating a {5}_____ album, sending a gift, poking {6}_____ user, indicating you "like" a {7}_____, attending an event, or connecting {8}_____ an application. In some cases {9}_____ are also taking an action {10}_____ you provide information or content {11}_____ us. For example, if you {12}_____ a video, in addition to {13}_____ the actual content you uploaded, {14}_____ might log the fact that {15}_____ shared it.

(To see the solution, turn the page.)

The full text—before inserting the blanks—scored at a 14th-grade reading level, corresponding to having completed two years of university. Thus if you're a typical, smart, college-educated reader, you can probably understand the paragraph and complete the Cloze test. Still, this is a higher reading level than what's required for much of the younger Facebook audience. Most teenage users need far easier text, and even college students prefer non-college level text when they're online—leisure sites shouldn't feel like textbooks.

Why Mobile Reading Is Challenging

User comprehension scores on the Cloze test were 48 percent of the desktop level when using the iPhone-sized screen. That is, it's roughly twice as hard to understand complicated content when reading on the smaller screen.

Why? In this case, people were reading only a single page of information, and they were shown that page as part of the study without having to find it. Thus navigation difficulties or other user interface issues cannot explain the increased difficulty. Also, users were tested in a lab, so there were no issues related to walking around with the phone or being disturbed by noises or other environmental events. (In the real world, such distractions and degradations of the user experience further reduce people's ability to understand mobile phone content during true mobile use.)

The only reason mobile scored lower than desktop is the screen size, because that was the only difference in the study conditions.

A smaller screen reduces comprehension for two reasons:

- Users can see less at any given time. Thus users must rely on their highly fallible memory when they are trying to understand anything that's not fully explained within the viewable space. Less context = less understanding.

- Users must move around the page more, scrolling to refer to other parts of the content instead of simply glancing at the text.

Scrolling introduces three problems:

- It takes more time, thus degrading memory.

- It diverts attention from the problem at hand to the secondary task of locating the required part of the page.

- It introduces the new problem of reacquiring the previous location on the page.

In **Figure 4.1** you can see an article from the app How Stuff Works. The article spreads across multiple screens; to follow the details in the text, users must remember or refer back to a diagram shown on a different screen.

Figure 4.1 The How Stuff Works app on iPhone: (**A**) Diagram of the different camera parts and (**B**) the explanation of how the camera works refers to the parts in the diagram. Users must go back to the diagram to understand the explanation.

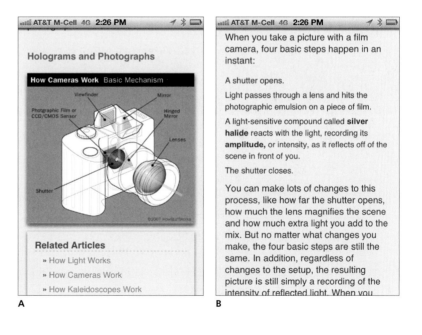

Figure 4.2 Lonely Planet's app for iPhone anchored the title of its article, thus reducing the effective screen space.

Because a small screen impairs comprehension, it's important to make sure that it's used optimally and not occupied with unnecessary or redundant information. For instance, Lonely Planet's choice (**Figure 4.2**) to make the title of the article sticky reduces the effective screen space without adding extra value to the user. Whereas this typically is recommended for e-commerce apps (where the "Buy now" button needs to be visible at all times in case users make up their mind as they scan through the product information—see Figure 4.11 and Figure 4.12 later in this chapter), it doesn't make sense for touring guide information. It makes even less sense when the title is as devoid of content as "Hello, Amsterdam" is. (See also Figure A.1 in the Appendix for an example of how we discovered this mobile design principle way back in 2000.)

Because comprehension is more difficult on mobile, it's imperative that mobile content be easy to read and scan. Roundabout, fluffy writing should be replaced with direct and concise content that is formatted for scannability.

Let's look at some examples of good and bad writing and formatting. In **Figure 4.3.**, Teavana is overly wordy and suffers from poor and buggy formatting: The *Health Info* paragraph has no punctuation and is preceded by the meaningless-to-the-user *FTGOP-2(SPECIAL)*.

Figure 4.3 (Left) Teavana app for iPhone: Tea description page. Not only is the description in the first paragraph relatively hard to read due to the multiple clauses per sentence and the many adjectives, but the formatting is buggy.

Figure 4.4 (Right) OSHA Heat Safety Tool app for Android.

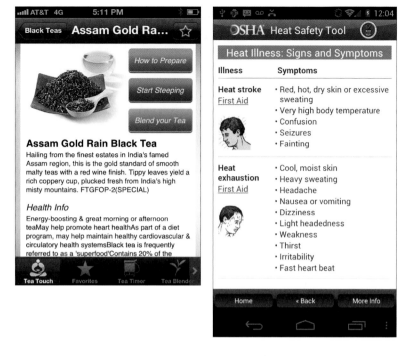

In contrast, OSHA (**Figure 4.4**) deserves a prize for concise, scannable writing for mobile: Emergency information needs to be read fast and understood easily, and the bullet points and keywords help with that. However the illustrations are just decorative: It is unlikely that they can help users identify the corresponding condition.

In general, bullet points make the information more scannable (**Figure 4.5**). In the Recalls.gov app (Figure 4.5A), the information is easy to read; the main points are bolded and attract the eye. (The use of the "previous" and "next" buttons at the top of the screen to navigate to a different article is less fortunate, because "next" and "previous" are low information-scent labels.) However too much space between bullet points can make the page look less structured, as in the HSN example (Figure 4.5B). Additionally, the table-without-borders format makes it hard for the user to know which description goes with each option. And the brand description under the first blue sentence is completely unnecessary on mobile: It does not focus on the product facts. Brand information is better delegated to a secondary page.

Figure 4.5 Bullets make the small page more scannable: (**A**) Recalls.gov app for Android and (**B**) HSN app for Android.

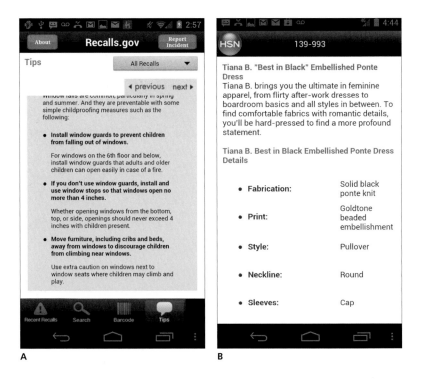

A

B

If in Doubt, Leave It Out

Our research on how users read on mobile devices has uncovered something of a paradox:

- Killing time is the killer app of mobile. As we've seen since our first mobile usability studies in 2000, killing time is the perfect match for mobile devices because they're readily available when users are waiting around for something to happen. Favorite time wasters include gossip, games, and sports. But even a seemingly serious task, like checking the stock market, is often no more than a time-killing episode in which users look up the current index numbers with no intent to trade.

- Mobile users are in a hurry and get visibly angry at verbose sites that waste their time. Also, it's twice as hard to understand content on small mobile devices as it is on bigger desktop screens, making wordy content even more despised.

How can people simultaneously want to kill time and get angry when their time is wasted? Well, that's a conundrum to be teased apart.

The solution to the puzzle lies in recognizing that even relaxation is purposeful behavior: According to information foraging theory (see the sidebar "Information Scent" in Chapter 3, "Designing for the Small Screen"), users seek to maximize their cost/benefit ratio. That is, people want *more* thrills and *less* interaction overhead.

Filler = Bad

Unfortunately interaction costs are inherently greater in mobile, which is why you need to focus mobile content even more tightly than content for desktop websites. **Figure 4.6** shows a typical example from one of our studies.

When reading the "breaking news" story about a tornado, one test user found commentary from local people and said, "*I don't need to know what everyone else is saying and the event from their point of view. I don't mind a quote from a local leader, but all this to me is just filler, and I wouldn't read it.*"

She went on to say, "*This is what came to me as breaking news? That's too much. It should be: This is what happened, and this is what's going on.*"

Several other test users made comments about not wanting to read entire news stories—especially "filler" content—on their phones. Users didn't want to bother with extra, secondary text, particularly in mobile apps designed for quick information consumption. They just wanted to know the main points.

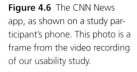

Figure 4.6 The CNN News app, as shown on a study participant's phone. This photo is a frame from the video recording of our usability study.

In all fairness, CNN has slightly changed its app since our testing, and now it has a summary (or "story highlights") at the beginning of the article that makes the article more scannable (**Figure 4.7**). It still doesn't fix the filler-information problem, but at least it makes it easier for the users to find the main points.

You might ask why people don't simply stop reading once they've consumed as much information as they want about a given topic. Sure, users do stop reading and are quick to leave sites. But they still feel drawn in by the writing and often skim more words than they really appreciate. And, after doing so, they feel duped because they didn't get sufficient payoff from investing their precious time.

There are two solutions:

- Cut the fluff. In particular, ditch the blah-blah verbiage that people inevitably place at the beginning of pages before getting to the meat of the matter. A good exercise is to simply delete your first paragraph and see if the page works as well without it. If it does, don't click that Undo button.

- Defer background material to secondary screens that are shown only to users who explicitly ask for more info. Such additional content supports people who have extra time on their hands or an exceptional interest in the topic.

Figure 4.7 A newer version of the CNN app for Android. The main story points are summarized at the beginning of the article.

The introductory paragraph(s) found at the top of many Web pages is what we call blah-blah text: a block of words that users typically skip when they arrive at a page. Instead their eyes go directly to more actionable content, such as product features, bulleted lists, or hypertext links.

The worst kind of blah-blah text has no function; it's pure filler—platitudes, such as "Welcome to our site, we hope you will find our new and improved design helpful."

Kill the welcome mat and cut to the chase.

Ruthlessly editing introductory paragraphs might be good advice, but why not just eliminate them completely? Cutting word count seems a weasely approach.

Some intro text serves a valid role in that it helps set the context for content and thus answer the question: What's the page about?

A brief introduction can help users better understand the rest of the page. Even if they skip it initially, they might return later if it doesn't look intimidatingly long and dense. If you keep it short, a bit of blah might actually work. So prune your initial draft of marketese and focus on answering two questions:

- **What?** (What will users find on this page— that is, what's its function?)
- **Why?** (Why should they care—that is, what's in it for them?)

When you're writing for mobile users, heed this maxim: If in doubt, leave it out.

Old Words Are Best

"Speak the user's language" has been a primary usability guideline for more than 20 years. The fact that the Web is a linguistic environment further increases the importance of using the right vocabulary.

In addition, mobile users are growing ever-more search dominant. Search is how people discover new websites and find individual pages within websites and intranets. Unless you're listed on the first search engine results page (SERP), you might as well not exist. So writing for the mobile Web is writing to be found.

There are many elements to search engine optimization (SEO), but SEO guideline #1 is our old friend, "Speak the user's language." Or, when you write, use keywords that match users' search queries.

Winston Churchill said that *"short words are best and the old words when short are best of all."* Churchill was talking about how to write punchy prose, not about SEO. To be found, precise words are often better than short words, which can be too broad to accurately describe the user's problem. For example, our audience is more likely to search for "usability" than for "easy".

But Churchill was right that old words are best.

Old words rule because people know them intimately. Familiar words spring to mind unbidden. Thus users are likely to employ old words when they boil down their problem to a search query, which is typically only two or three words long—particularly on mobile where it's hard to type.

Because old words are used most frequently, people understand them faster. Remember that on mobile, users are often rushed and text comprehension is difficult. Using familiar and precise words delivers the gist of the content more quickly and makes it less likely for users to need to refer back to other parts of your text. **Figure 4.8** shows an example of hard-to-read text that relies heavily on economic jargon (from the app Labor Stats). You could perhaps argue that this app is for an audience with some sort of economic education. If so, such an audience is probably fairly versed in the economic lingo and needs neither a vague definition of "labor productivity" ("relationship between output and labor time"—what is the nature of this relationship and how is it calculated?) nor a more precise one.

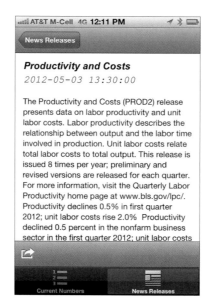

Figure 4.8 The Labor Stats app for iPhone. The news release in this app has been rewritten for mobile, but the use of economic jargon (as well as the lack of formatting) makes it hard to read and hard to follow.

Bylines for Mobile Content?

Should you identify the author of articles and other website content? Or should the material remain anonymous and be published under the organization's institutional voice?

Unfortunately there's no single answer to the Web bylines question. But there are a number of criteria, some that follow the mobile writing principle discussed earlier—cut the fluff.

Against bylines: Cut the fluff

Here are the reasons to remove bylines:

- As always when writing for online use—and particularly for mobile—one main guideline is to keep it short. Users spend very little time on Web pages; information that doesn't provide sufficient value-added should be left out. On average, users read only about 120 words per page view, so you may not want three of those few words to be "*by Joe Schmoe.*"

- Mobile copy should be cut even more than you might cut verbiage for a desktop site. Even if some of the following criteria lead you to include bylines, it might be better to remove them for the mobile version of your site.

For bylines: Establish credibility

Bylines can be worth their word count in the following cases:

- **If the author is famous**—maybe even famous enough that people might read the piece mainly to hear what he or she has to say on some current issue. In this case, you should include the author's name when linking to the article from homepages, SERPs, article listings, tweets, and so on.

  Note that "fame" doesn't necessarily equate to "celebrity." Respected geeks can be well known in specialized communities while being completely unknown to 99 percent of the population. What counts is whether the author is known to the target audience.

- **If the author has credentials or status that support the article's credibility.** The classic example is a medical doctor writing about a health issue, in which case you should certainly list the article as being "*by Joe Schmoe, MD.*"

- **If the author has experience that provides some credibility.** For example, the designer of a website should be named when you're writing an article discussing that design.

- **If the author often writes about a certain topic.** Regular readers might recognize the name and want to seek out the writer's other articles.

Usually a brief author biography is secondary content that should appear on a separate page. However if a credentialed or experienced author's credibility-boosting effect requires more info than just his or her name, you should add a one-line bio abstract at the top of the page to encourage users to read the article. (For example, *"by Dr. Joe Schmoe, head of the Cystic Fibrosis Centre, Toronto Hospital for Sick Children"* in an article about Cystic Fibrosis in children.)

Longer biographies should always be relegated to secondary pages and linked from the author's name. But don't link the name to an email address for two reasons:

- It's distracting for users when clicking a name initiates an email instead of showing a new Web page, which is the expected behavior of Web links.
- Users are much more likely to want to *read* about the author than to *contact* the author. If appropriate, you can add contact info at the bottom of the biography page.

Author biographies should include a portrait photo, at least when you provide a separate bio page. This can be a standard headshot or an action shot of the author doing something relevant to the article (such as sitting on a tractor for a farmer writing about farming).

Also the author bio page should include links to the author's other articles on the site, except in the case of weblogs or other sites that are essentially the work of a single author.

- **If the article is an opinion piece, review, political commentary, or other type of content that is specifically positioned as an individual person's take on an issue.** A byline is needed simply to clarify the content's status. Depending on the nature of the site, such content might also require a disclaimer that the analysis does not necessarily represent the organization's position.

- **If the article belongs to an intranet.** Naming authors can help establish a feeling of community by helping employees get to know each other.

Here are some examples of situations where bylines are or are not appropriate on mobile. Zite, a news aggregator (**Figure 4.9**), justifiably uses bylines indicating the source of the different articles. On the other hand, including author information in the article listings (like ProPublica in **Figure 4.10A**) is not warranted. That prime real estate should be used for more important information. The *Washington Post* (**Figure 4.10B**) lists the article author on the article page beneath the title. Although better than listing it on the headline page, it still takes up valuable space; it would be best if that space were used for content unless the *Washington Post* has some reason to believe that this author is famous enough for people to seek his articles. (The top of the page tends to get the most attention and should be reserved for essential information.) If the author needs to be credentialed and is not famous, consider adding the name at the end of the article—as in the CNN *Money* example in **Figure 4.10C**.

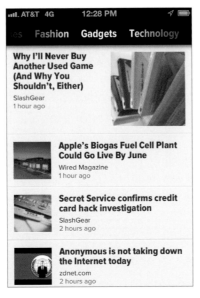

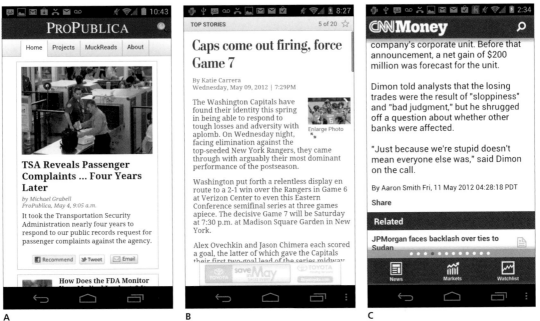

Figure 4.10 Author bylines are not necessary on mobile: (**A**) ProPublica's website (propublica.org); (**B**) *Washington Post* app for Android; and (**C**) CNN *Money* app for Android.

Defer Secondary Information to Secondary Screens

Our own studies of mobile usability have found that users are typically rushed when using their mobile devices. A contrasting mobile use case is people who simply want to kill time while waiting. However most tasks are at least somewhat goal directed, and people using a mobile device often have minimal time to accomplish them. For example, when you check email on your phone, you tend to allocate less time to a newsletter than you would when reading email at home or in the office.

We've known since 1997 that it's best to be concise when writing for the Web. Mobile simply reinforces this point and stretches it to the limit. Short is too long for mobile. Ultrashort rules the day.

How can you be super-concise and still offer the info people need? You do that by deferring secondary information to secondary screens. The first screen users see should be ruthlessly focused on the minimum information needed to communicate your top point.

Example 1: Mobile Coupons

Discount coupons are a perfect mobile service because they're highly dependent on time and/or location: Flash sales have a sense of urgency because people want to know about a coupon before it sells out. Similarly people are likely to be interested in coupons for shops and products they encounter while they're out and about (and away from their desktop computers).

Figure 4.11 shows an example of how a Groupon deal looks on an Android phone.

The initial view is clearly suited for the hurried mobile user. The detailed view, on the other hand, is a nice second step for people who are really interested, but it would have been a great turnoff to show this wall of text as the first screen.

Groupon worked well in our mobile usability study. Groupon changed its design slightly, so that now "More about this deal" actually appears on the same page (**Figure 4.12**). It kept the nicely structured information at the top of the page. The new design is still layered, but instead of moving the details on a separate page, it puts them on the same page at the bottom.

A competing service, LivingSocial, did poorly, as shown in **Figure 4.13**.

Figure 4.11 Mobile Groupon deal: (**A**) initial view and (**B**) detail view. You get the detailed view when you select "More about this deal" on the first screen.

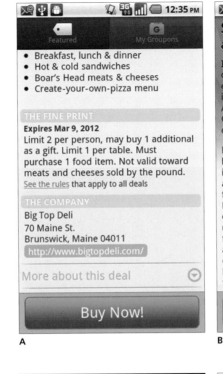

A

If left unfulfilled, stomachs express discontent with growls emphatic enough to draw stares on the train and instigate fights with stray wolverines. Avoid tummy tussles with today's Groupon: for $6, you get $12 worth of deli fare at Big Top Deli.

Big Top Deli fuels empty tanks with a bounty of breakfast, lunch, and dinner items, employing Boar's Head meats and cheeses to offer customers a flavorful cornucopia of deli delights. Manage morning pangs while expressing infatuation with sparsely used letters by ordering a Zazel, which fuses an egg with provolone, prosciutto, and roasted red peppers ($4). Afternoon cravings are toppled with a variety of both cold and hot sandwiches, ranging from classic turkey clubs ($7.25) to the

Buy Now!

B

Figure 4.12 On the newer version of Groupon, all the text under "More about this deal" appears at the bottom of the page.

Figure 4.13 Mobile LivingSocial: Sample deal.

LivingSocial offends against several mobile usability guidelines. Cute babies are always nice, but in a mobile user interface, stock photos only push salient information off the small screen. With this layout and writing, it's hard to find out what you're buying. And if there's one thing we know about mobile users, it's that they are usually too busy to work at finding information.

(In fairness to LivingSocial, the "Buy Now" button does follow guidelines for easy touchability on a mobile screen: It's big, clear, and has nothing near it that users might tap by mistake.)

Here's what two of our study participants said about these two ways of presenting coupon offers on mobile devices:

- **LivingSocial's presentation:** *"It just seems like more of a display that would be on a website as opposed to adapting it on the phone. It would be fine to me if it was on my computer."* The same user on the Groupon app: *"It's the quick version on the front. There are options to see more, but there isn't a ton of info. Since it's a phone, crowding the screen isn't a good idea."*

- **Another user on Groupon:** *"I like the really quick bulleted format."* And on LivingSocial: *"You have to read through the whole thing to see what's included in it."*

Example 2: Progressive Disclosure in Wikipedia

Wikipedia has always had two qualities: extensive hypertext linking and exhaustive content, telling you something about everything. Wikipedia has also always exemplified bad writing, with contributors who have little insight into a topic's truly important aspects and thus have an inability to prioritize information in their articles.

Given this decade-long tradition, we were somewhat surprised that Wikipedia scored well for information prioritization in our study. **Figure 4.14** shows an example of how an article looks the first time users see it on their phones.

This design focuses users nicely on the article's key points while deferring secondary information. The page starts by showing the main biographical facts in a tabular format, followed by a short paragraph about Dr. Huang and collapsed sections that contain further details. Of course this is nothing but a case of progressive disclosure, which is a very old idea in human–computer interaction (see the sidebar "Progressive Disclosure" in Chapter 3). This established design principle comes to the forefront when you're writing for mobile.

Figure 4.14 Mobile Wikipedia (m.wikipedia.org): (**A**) initial article view and (**B**) information visible by scrolling down the page.

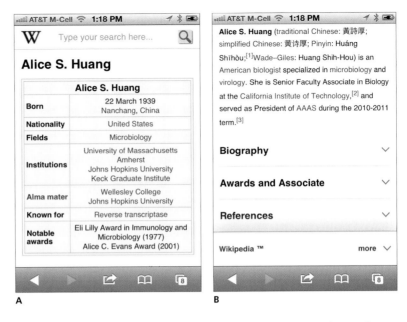

It's particularly effective to show an outline of the secondary information instead of dumping it into a linear scrolling page. Users can immediately see, for example, that there's a section about awards. And if they care about awards, they can expand this section without having to slog their way through a long biography section.

Here's what some of our test users said about mobile Wikipedia:

- *"It's sort of giving me an outline. They have their TOCs at the top, so it gives you the headings but not the whole thing. So you know what the heads are in the article and go to them as you wish."*

- *"I like that* [hiding content] *better than having everything available. I can open the bio and not see all the references. It's something I appreciate."*

Of course, in true obsessive-compulsive Wikipedia fashion, this article also includes material that's definitely not well written for mobile. The table at the beginning of the page does contain information that may be considered less important (for example, where Dr. Huang studied). And, given that users are likely interested in understanding Dr. Huang's scientific accomplishments, explaining how her name would be transcribed in Pinyin and Wades-Giles is not even secondary information; it's tertiary at best and, on mobile, should have been delegated to a secondary layer.

Deferring Information = Initial Info Read More

It's a tough decision to defer most of your information to secondary screens because many users will never see it, even though you no doubt consider it very important.

But remember: if you make the first screen too dense, *nobody* will read anything. It's better to focus the initial screen and let those users who're particularly interested dig into the rest. That way you'll satisfy more customers, get more traffic, and derive more business value from your mobile content.

Figure 4.15 shows an example of good information layering from Apple. The software update information is presented very briefly on the main page; those few users who are interested in more details can click the link "Learn More" and get the extras on a secondary page. (The wording "Learn More," however, is less than ideal, because it does not carry much information scent and is one of the more salient items on the page.)

Figure 4.15 Software update on Apple iPhone: (**A**) main page and (**B**) detail page. The information is layered.

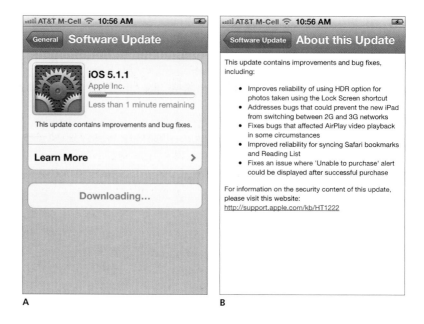

A   B

News sites often offer another example of good layering (**Figure 4.16**): Many users are able to get the information they need quickly by scanning the article summary on the headline page rather than reading the entire article. For that reason, "true" summaries (like those from The *Wall Street Journal* in Figure 4.16A) that make sense on their own and capture the gist of the story are preferable to sentence fragments (as *USA Today* uses in Figure 4.16B) or to just echoing the first sentence of the article.

Figure 4.16 Summaries for articles in a list of headlines are an example of layered content. (**A**) The *Wall Street Journal's* website (m.wsj.com) and (**B**) *USA Today* app for Android.

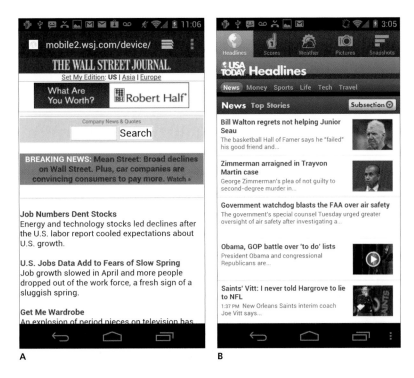

A B

However some companies push the layering too far, to the extent of forcing *all* users to go to a secondary page to find *any* information. **Figure 4.17** shows two examples (WebMD and Net-a-porter) that manage to show practically zero useful information on the first page, forcing users to tap again to get to the relevant details.

In the WebMD app (Figure 4.17A–B) the main types of information pertaining to the drug are easy to scan; however the page is arguably too structured. It would have been preferable to have a brief summary under each of the different sections (uses, side effects, etc.), so that users could quickly get the main idea and then move to more information if they wanted to. Once users click to any of the sections (in [b]), they get to a page only barely formatted for mobile: The lack of bullet points makes that page hard to scan.

Net-a-porter (Figure 4.17C–D) also forces the users to tap for information about a product. Only the image is displayed on the main product page; all the other relevant details are sent to secondary screens. That information should all be present explicitly on the page with links to only that info that most users would not need (for example, "What size I am"). The essential content, relevant to most people, needs to be on the first screen in a scannable and concise format, and not be delegated to a secondary screen.

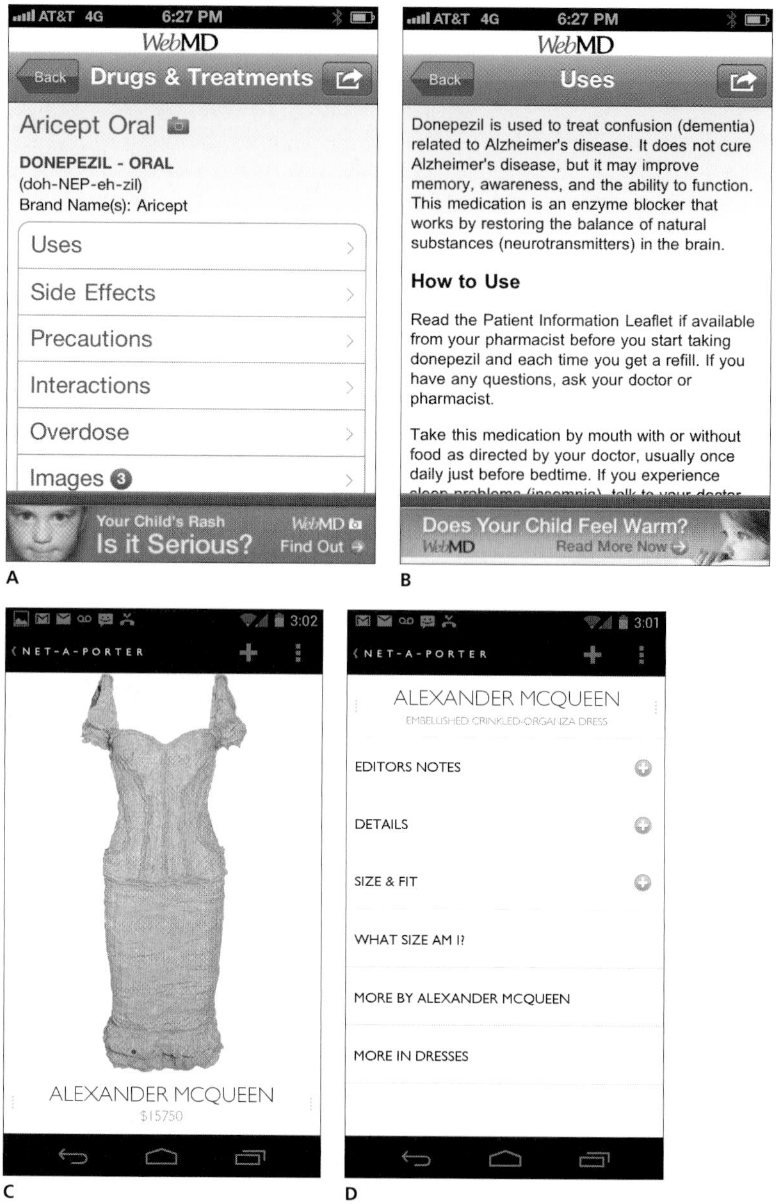

Figure 4.17 Information structured into sections: (**A**)–(**B**) WebMD for iPhone and (**C**)–(**D**) Net-a-porter for Android. Both apps display too little information on the main page.

Mini-IA: Structuring Content

The definition of mini-information architecture (mini-IA) is simple: It's how you structure the information about a single topic. For example, the mini-IA of an email message is a single page.

When something is covered on a single page, we don't usually think of the presentation as "information architecture." However the very decision to stick to a single-page format is an IA matter.

Often it's better to break up information into multiple units rather than using an overly long linear flow, like that shown in **Figure 4.18**. You can then present these multiple units across a few pages or use a within-page navigation system, such as tabs or carousels.

Linear Paging? Usually Bad

Let's first dismiss a popular mini-IA as being almost universally bad for usability: If you have a long article, it's almost never good to do as NBC does in the example in **Figure 4.19** and simply chop it up into a linear sequence of pages. If the only navigation is a "Continue" or "Next page" link, it's typically better to stick it all on a single page and rely on scrolling instead of page turning. Not only do users have to wait for a page to load every half a minute or so, but should they want to go back to the list of episodes when they finish reading the summary, they would need to tap the browser's Back button 12 times.

Figure 4.18 Ted Video for iPhone. All the 104 available videos are presented in a long list. A mini-IA grouping of videos on topics would have been more helpful.

Figure 4.19 NBC's mobile website (m.nbc.com) splits episode summaries into many pages with just a picture and a paragraph per page.

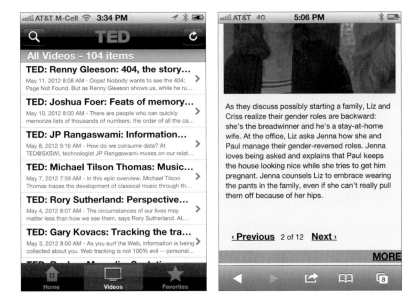

(The exception here is for content presented on tablets, such as the iPad, or for book-reader apps where the swiping gesture provides a generic command for moving between pages and/or the content is preloaded, so it doesn't take any time to move between pages. Also, books are not usually read in a single session, and having the book split into pages makes it easier for users to keep their place in the book; otherwise, imagine having to scroll through an entire book to find the third paragraph in Chapter 11.)

In many situations the best alternative is to chunk information into individual content units, focusing on logical cohesiveness. You can then describe each unit accordingly and let users navigate directly to the unit that meets their needs. (Note that "page 2 of 12" is neither descriptive nor deserving of its own page.)

(For wizard-style interactions, such as e-commerce checkout, a linear page-turning progression usually works better because even though each step is logically cohesive, they're in an application workflow, so you can't go to step 3 without first completing step 2.)

Alphabetical Sorting Must (Mostly) Die

Another popular mini-IA that is often misused is alphabetical ordering. Sorting a list of options alphabetically has two main benefits:

- If users know the name of what they want, they can usually find it in the list pretty quickly.

- Lazy design teams don't have to work on figuring out a better structure. Because we all know our ABCs, anybody can put the items into the correct sequence.

The first point is a true benefit, and alphabetical sorting works fine in some cases. For example, it's usually easy enough to pick out a state from an alphabetical list of the 50 U.S. states. Indeed, in this case an alpha listing is more usable than, say, grouping the states by region or showing them on a map—at least when users need to click only one state (usually their own) to navigate to a page with state-related information.

(Listing states alphabetically is a good choice only when people have to select one state from a menu for navigation or a command. When users need to specify the state as part of their address—as in e-commerce checkout forms—it's better to present a text field where people can type the two-letter abbreviation. This is faster and less error prone; on mobile, it also avoids the need for prolonged scrolling within a small drop-down box that spans only half of the tiny Phone screen, as in **Figure 4.20**.)

Figure 4.20 Macy's app for iPhone. Selecting a state from a drop-down box is inefficient.

Lists of countries and other known-item problems are also often fine to alphabetize. However you do need to ensure that users will know *unambiguously* the name of their selection. If people have to look at several places in the list, you've defeated the purpose of the A–Z order.

For most questions, either:

- Users don't know the name of what they want, making A–Z listings useless,

    or

- The items have an inherent logic that dictates a different sort order, which makes A–Z listings directly harmful because they hide that logic.

Sizes are ordinal data, meaning that they have an inherent monotonically increasing sequence. Such items should almost always be sorted accordingly.

Other times, items have domain-related logical groupings. You can often determine this underlying logic in a card-sorting study where you ask users to group related items together.

For example, Epicurious is a recipe app that allows users to search and save recipes (**Figure 4.21**). The list of favorite (or saved) recipes can be seen in alphabetical order or in recently added order. Neither works for a long list of recipes. In the case of alphabetical sorting, the first word of a recipe name (such as, "Balsamic" for "Balsamic roasted vegetables") is often nonindicative of the recipe. And except for very recent recipes, users are unlikely to remember when they've added a recipe to their list for the first time. (To add insult to injury, Epicurious does not have a search function for the recipe box, making it very difficult for people to deal with a large number of recipes.) A mini-IA that grouped recipes under different categories (fish, meat, desserts, etc.) would have been a lot more useful.

Timelines and geographical location are other groupings that are often useful, although sometimes they can go wrong, too, as shown in the example in **Figure 4.22**. The entries in the list are geographical locations, but the editors had their own understanding of alphabetical order: The Black Forest is under "F" (presumably for "Forest"), and Antwerp is under "G" (for "Geography of Antwerp"). It's very unlikely that users could guess at this type of classification; in fact, when searching for Antwerp, they'll probably just stop at "A," thinking that it shouldn't appear farther down the "alphabetically" ordered list.

Figure 4.21 Epicurious for iPhone. The list of favorite recipes can be sorted in alphabetical order or in recently added order. Neither of these is appropriate for long lists of recipes.

Figure 4.22 How Stuff Works app for iPhone. Here's an example of alphabetical order gone wrong: Antwerp is under "G" (for "Geography of Antwerp").

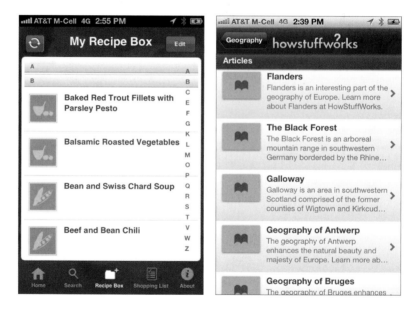

You can let the importance or frequency of use guide how you prioritize long listings rather than default to less-useful alphabetical sorting.

Depending on the nature of your information, usability might be better served by yet other types of structures. And yes, in a few cases, this might even be the alphabet. But typically, when you reach for an A–Z structure, you should give yourself a little extra kick and seek out something better.

Example: Usage-relevant Structure

To illustrate a usage-relevant structure, look at **Figure 4.23**, which shows two example structures that present information about exercises in a mobile fitness app.

Figure 4.23 Lists of exercises in two iPhone apps: (**A**) You Are Your Own Gym and (**B**) Full Fitness.

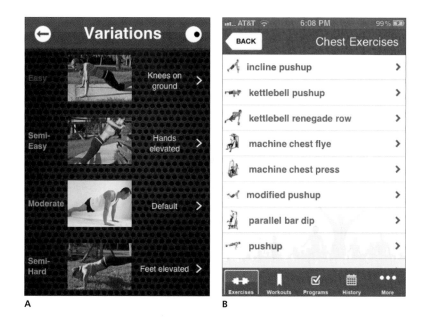

A   B

The example in Figure 4.23A employs a useful mini-IA for push-up exercises: It puts all the exercises together in a list that's ordered from the easiest to the hardest. In contrast, the example in Figure 4.23B sorts the exercises alphabetically, which, as discussed in the previous section, is usually a poor structure.

The Full Fitness screen shot (Figure 4.23B) shows only a part of the complete list and includes incline push-up, modified push-up, and plain old push-up. How do you know which one to pick if you want a variation that's a bit more challenging than your last exercise? Is "modified" easy or difficult?

"Modified" obviously emits poor information scent: The word tells you what the exercise is *not* instead of what it *is*. "Incline" is better, though not as clear as the equivalent "hands elevated" label used by You Are Your Own Gym. Quick, what's the difference between an incline push-up and a decline push-up? We bet you can't answer that as quickly (or as correctly) as you might decipher "hands elevated" versus "feet elevated." Simpler words are usually best. (You're excused from preferring simple words if you're writing for an expert audience. But advanced fitness enthusiasts definitely won't need to look up how to perform an incline push-up, even if that's what they might prefer calling this exercise.)

The designers of Full Fitness would have surely benefited from reading this chapter. That said, their main problem is structural. Even with improved labels, the current Full Fitness scheme would remain less usable than the You Are Your Own Gym solution, which recognizes that push-up variations deserve their own mini-IA structured according to the best way to make sense of different push-up exercises (here, progressing from easy to hard as you get stronger).

As an aside, both apps use thumbnail photos to further explain the exercises and help users determine which one to choose. And both have usability problems. Except for the "moderate" photo, You Are Your Own Gym's photos have too much background detail to be easily understood given their small size. Full Fitness's photos are cleaner and almost as easy to grasp as the Own Gym photos, even though they're much smaller. We usually criticize tiny thumbnails, but most of the Full Fitness images (except for the two machine exercises) are clean enough to adequately differentiate the exercises.

Another example of good mini-IA comes from Teavana (**Figure 4.24**). Teavana splits its teas by type (white, green, oolong, and black). Interestingly, Teavana implements its mini-IA in a slightly different way than You Are Your Own Gym (see Figure 4.23A): Teavana's mini-IA is

Figure 4.24 Teavana app for iPhone. Teavana appropriately uses a mini-IA for its tea list. The top panel with the four types of teas is persistent.

not given a separate page; instead it's shown in a persistent strip (that doesn't disappear as the user scrolls down through the list of teas) at the top of the tea list. This solution sacrifices some screen space, but it lets users change the tea type more efficiently. However the thumbnails are small and hardly necessary: It's unlikely that anybody would recognize or select a tea using that kind of image (or, perhaps, any image at all.)

Usage-driven Structure

When you have a lot of information about a topic, there are three ways of presenting it:

- **One long page.** One long page is a simple choice but makes it harder for users to access individual subtopics. You also risk intake fatigue as users slog their way through the page to the bitter end (and many will give up before the going gets too bitter).

- **Mini-IA.** Mini-IA lets you split the info into appropriate chunks. This allows direct access to subtopics of interest and can give users a better understanding of the concept space than they'd get while putting their nose to the grindstone to endlessly scroll.

- **Distributed information.** Distributed information lets you blend together subtopics of many topics, as in the push-up exercises, cable machine exercises, and so on in the Full Fitness section on "Chest Exercises" (Figure 4.23B).

Here we've argued that usability is often enhanced by the second approach. However, a mini-IA makes sense only if you can structure this localized information space according to a principle that supports the users' tasks and mental models.

Since the Web's beginning, internally focused structuring has been one of the most user-repellent design mistakes. Our research into intranet IA, for example, has repeatedly found that both usage and employee productivity skyrocket when a department-based IA is replaced by a task-based IA.

Along similar lines, a mini-IA won't help if it's structured according to your internal organizational chart or any other way that fails to match how customers want to access information. But if you embrace a mini-IA—identifying a usage-based structuring scheme as a basis for a clear and modest navigation system—you'll likely have a winner on your hands.

5 Tablets and E-readers

Moving from smartphones to tablets may seem like a small step—a difference of screen size. But although many design recommendations for smartphones stay true for tablets, the size difference dictates usage differences as well as design differences. In this chapter we explore the usability of the iPad and the Kindle Fire as the most interesting exponents of large-screen tablets and midsize tablets, respectively. We also briefly discuss Kindle Fire's ancestor, the Kindle e-reader.

iPad Usability

"It looks like a giant iPhone" is the first remark from users when they are asked to test an iPad. (Their second comment? *"Wow, it's heavy."*)

But from an interaction design perspective, an iPad UI (user interface) shouldn't be a scaled-up iPhone UI. **Figure 5.1** shows Alfred, an app that learns your restaurant preferences and recommends new ones. Alfred has the same interface on the iPad and iPhone. This is an easy solution, but not one that we recommend. Whereas the iPhone version is crowded, the iPad version wastes the available screen space.

Not only does the iPad have a bigger screen, but, equally important, the context of its use is different. Much noise has been made about the assertion that the iPad is not mobile; the truth is that it is and it isn't. Although people may carry their iPads with them, there is less pressure of an immediate, local response that users expect from their smartphones.

Figure 5.1 Alfred has the same interface on the iPad and iPhone: (**A**) Alfred for iPhone and (**B**) Alfred for iPad.

A big difference between the iPad and iPhone is that regular websites work reasonably well on the big tablet (**Figure 5.2**). The text on the full site is fairly readable on the iPad, although some of the targets may be quite small and difficult to touch. As long as users don't need to complete complex tasks, focusing on reading and looking at pictures or video are relatively easy. The mobile site, on the other hand, looks sparse and impoverished on the iPad; the full site seems to take better advantage of the space. In contrast, our iPhone usability studies show that users strongly prefer using apps rather than the full Web. It's simply too painful to use most websites on the small screen. (Mobile-optimized sites alleviate this issue, but usually even they have worse usability than apps—see our discussion in the section "Mobile Sites vs. Apps: The Coming Strategy Shift" in Chapter 2, "Mobile Strategy.")

Still, on the iPad most Web pages offer a rich and overstuffed experience compared to the iPad's sparse and regulated environment; when an iPad app suddenly teleports users into the Web, the transition can be jarring.

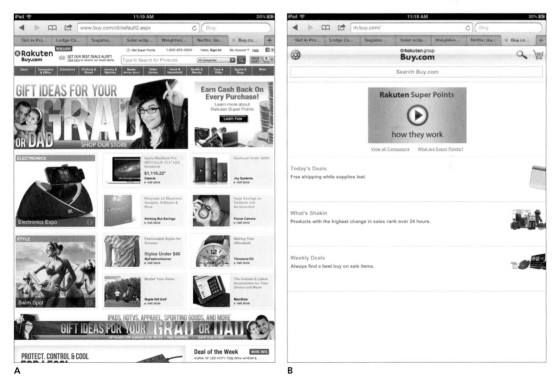

A **B**

Figure 5.2 Buy.com on the iPad: (**A**) the full site and (**B**) the mobile site.

And, of course, there's still the "fat finger" problem common to all touch screens, which makes it difficult for users to tap small targets reliably. The iPad has a read–tap asymmetry where text *big enough* to read is *too small* to touch. Thus we definitely recommend large touch zones on any Web page hoping to attract many iPad users.

We did see some Web pages that worked well on tablets, because they had bigger touchable areas. For example, Virgin America's reservation page (**Figure 5.3**) lets users touch anywhere in the entire table cell containing a desired departure, as opposed to having to touch the much smaller area represented by the radio button (or even its label). Those targets work well on the iPad. (However not all pages on Virgin America's site are iPad-friendly: Some of the targets—including, for instance, the radio buttons for showing fares in U.S. dollars or Elevate Points—are still too small.)

Figure 5.3 Virgin America's website (virginamerica.com): The reservation page has big, padded targets in the table that requires users to select a flight.

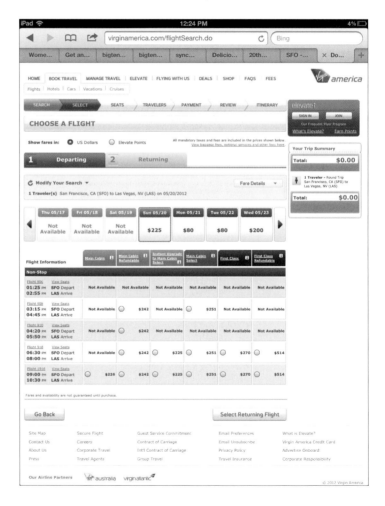

For more than a decade, when we've asked users for their first impression of (desktop) websites, the most frequently used word has been "busy." In contrast, the first impression of many iPad apps is "beautiful" (**Figure 5.4**). Newer iPads benefit from higher-resolution ("retina") displays that enable even stronger visual experiences. Small, hard to decipher pictures don't take full advantage of iPad's propensity for beautiful images—as testified by the contrast between the poor-quality thumbnails in **Figure 5.5A** and the bigger, clearer ones in **Figure 5.5B**.

The change to a more soothing user experience (UX) is certainly welcome, especially for a device that may turn out to be more of a leisure computer than a business computer. Still, beauty shouldn't come at the cost of being able to actually use the apps and derive real benefits from their features and content.

In just two years since the iPad was introduced, iPad usability is much improved, and people habitually use many apps. As always, this is no reason to relax your vigilance; new usability problems have appeared and the old ones haven't been totally vanquished. Mainly, though, the future is bright for touch-driven tablet UX.

Figure 5.4 The Elements app on the iPad is a coffee-table book that migrated into an app. Users were often amazed at the beauty of the images.

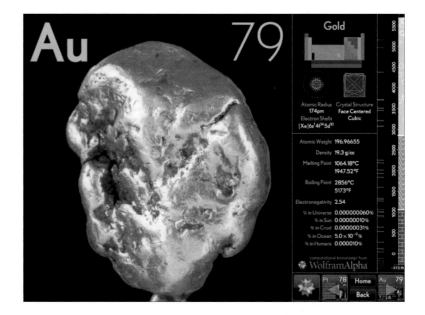

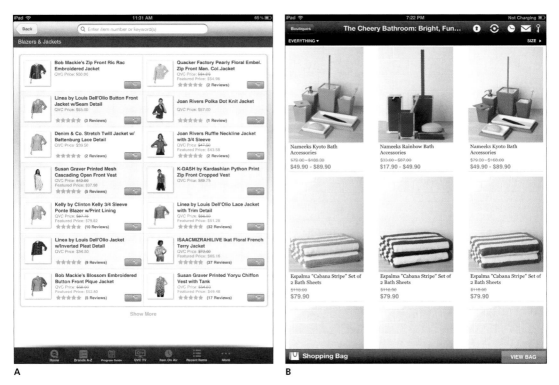

Figure 5.5 Images are a strength of the iPad. (**A**) The QVC app uninspiredly prioritizes text over product images. (**B**) Rue La La, a flash-sale app, uses big and inviting product thumbnails.

Tablets Are Shared Devices

Except for those who lived alone, our study participants uniformly reported sharing their iPads with other family members. When we asked them to walk us through the apps on their tablet, people frequently came across apps that someone else in their family had installed.

The iPad's shared nature contrasts with the much more personal nature of mobile phones, which are typically owned and used by single individuals.

Obviously tablets might become truly personal devices in the future as competition drives down the prices. But for now you should assume that you're designing for a multiuser device. For example, users might be reluctant to stay permanently signed in to an app, and they'll still forget their passwords. It's also important to design recognizable application icons so they'll stand out in the crowded listings of several users' apps.

What Are iPads Used For?

About half of our users reported that they carry their iPads with them frequently; the other half said they use them mainly at home or on longer trips.

The most common uses recounted by our participants were playing games, checking email and social networking sites, watching videos/movies, and reading news. People also browsed the Web and performed some shopping-related research. But most users felt that it was easier to shop on their desktop computers. Some also worried about the security of e-commerce purchases on the iPad.

We often hear users saying that the iPad has replaced their laptop. That does not mean that they suddenly started coding or creating PowerPoint presentations on their iPad, but some of the more complex information-finding tasks are migrating from the laptop to the iPad. Users may attempt to research vacation destinations or new products on the iPad, whether they decide to make a purchase on the spot or not. Most users don't even think of doing such a task on the smartphone; instead, they might limit themselves to simple, contextual information needs, such as finding the closest hotel if they got stuck in a snow storm.

Generally iPad use is heavily dominated by media *consumption*, except for the small amount of *production* involved in responding to emails. Indeed, killing time (which often involves some sort of media consumption) is the other major use for both smartphones and tablets. Killing time is often device-driven rather than user-driven: The user may have a very general goal (for example, read news, browse through a magazine) and is happy to digest roughly whatever content the device is offering. However, even for killing time, the use patterns for phones versus tablets are slightly different: The smartphone sessions are much shorter and more fragmented than those on the iPad. On the smartphone, users may look for a quick article to kill three minutes while waiting for the train; once on the train, they may take out the iPad for the hour it takes them to ride home.

As one user put it when referring to his iPad, *"I am not in a rush when I use this device."*

The Triple Threat of iPad Design

iPad UIs can easily fall prey to a triple threat that causes significant user confusion:

- **Low discoverability.** The UI is mostly hidden within the etched-glass aesthetic without perceived affordances. See the side-bar "Perceived Affordance: Can You See Me Now?" Areas don't look touchable.

- **Low memorability.** Gestures are inherently ephemeral and difficult to learn when they're not employed consistently across apps. Wider reliance on generic commands as discussed in Chapter 3, "Designing for the Small Screen," would help.

- **Accidental activation.** This occurs when users touch things by mistake or make a gesture that unexpectedly initiates a feature. Unintended touches caused trouble again and again, particularly in apps lacking a Back button.

Low discoverability and affordances

The first crop of iPad apps revived memories of Web designs from 1993 when Mosaic first introduced the image map that made it possible for *any* part of *any* picture to become a UI element. As a result, graphic designers went wild: Anything they could draw could be a UI, whether it made sense or not.

It was the same with the first iPad apps: Anything you could show and touch could be a UI on this device. The prevailing aesthetic was very much that of flat images that filled the screen as if they were etched, with no visual distractions or nerdy buttons. The penalty for this beauty was the reemergence of a usability problem we haven't seen since the mid-1990s: Users didn't know where they could click (or tap).

In the last 15 years of Web usability research, the main problems have been that users don't know where to *go* or which option to *choose*—not that they don't even know which options exist. With the early iPad UIs, we were back to this square one: Often there were no perceived affordances for how various screen elements responded when touched.

In contrast, long-standing GUI design guidelines for desktop user designs dictate that buttons look raised (and thus pressable), and that scroll bars and other interactive elements are visually distinct from the content.

The traditional GUI separation between "church and state"—that is, between content and features or commands—has carried over to modern Web design. Those 1993-style image maps are long gone from any site that hopes to do business on the Internet.

Today iPad standards are beginning to emerge, but we still see apps that lack affordances. The Martha Stewart Cocktails app in **Figure 5.6** buries the navigation bar under a low-affordance ribbon in the top-left corner and lets users guess where the navigation might be. In the same app, the color red is used interchangeably for content that is tappable or not (for instance, "Frozen Bloody Mary" and "Serves 4" are not tappable, but "Share" and "Add" are).

Similarly the Star Trek PADD app (**Figure 5.7**) does a poor job of signaling tappability and also suffers from lack of consistency in rendering touch affordances. The search tool is hidden under the "Search" text at the bottom of the screen on the right; that text does not look touchable. One reason is that it's surrounded by icons and other oval-enclosed strings in the navigation bar at the bottom of the screen. If those are tappable (and they are), then anything else that's tappable should look like them.

Although some designs do a better job of conveying functionality in the interface and guiding the users, there is still the attraction of zero chrome, and many apps still assume that users will joyfully explore their app and discover features (**Figure 5.8**). (For an in-depth discussion of chrome, see the section "Chrome" in Chapter 3.)

Figure 5.6 Martha Stewart Cocktails for iPad. The ribbon/logo in the top-left corner hides a navigation bar. Unfortunately the ribbon lacks touch affordance.

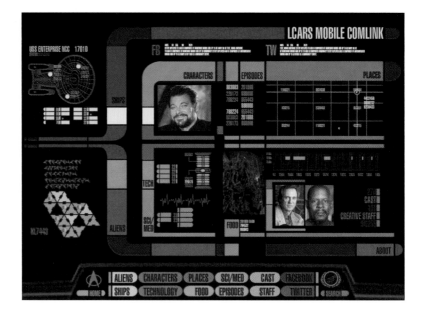

Figure 5.7 The Star Trek PADD app for iPad. The blue "Search" text at the bottom of the screen on the right does not look tappable, but it is (as is the symmetrical "Home" string on the left side of the screen).

Figure 5.8 The *New York Times'* The Collection for iPad uses big photographs at the expense of text.

In Figure 5.8, The Collection for iPad collects fashion–related stories from the *New York Times*. The app attempts to take advantage of the appeal of photographs on the iPad. The stories are presented as big thumbnails with no text visible. When users tap on one of the thumbnails, they can read a summary of the story. To read the entire story or see a larger version of the picture, users must tap again on one of the icons displayed below the summary. Even in a fashion-related, photograph-intensive app, it's difficult to figure out what the story is about just by looking at the thumbnail. And the summary presented on a busy background is challenging to read.

Low memorability and gestures

We discussed gestures and their memorability in Chapter 3 when we talked about the attempt to get away from chrome by using gestures. Because the iPad allows multifinger gestures that were not possible on its predecessor, the iPhone, there was an explosion of interest in using gestures, and even defining new gestures, to make the experience more immersive.

However gestures have no perceived affordance, and people cannot easily guess them. Even if the apps tell users what they are supposed to do, new gestures are cumbersome and users often have a hard time replicating them reliably.

Perceived Affordance: Can You See Me Now?

The term *affordance* simply means what you can do with something. Classic examples are that a button affords pushing, whereas a dial affords turning. A chair mainly affords sitting but maybe also standing—if you want to reach a high shelf without bothering to get a ladder.

On a touch screen, any single point obviously affords touching, tapping, sliding your finger, moving your finger in a zigzag pattern, or any other gesture. In theory, that is—you could *try* each of these movements, but would anything happen?

In practice, we call something an affordance in a user interface only if that action is not just possible, but also recognized by the system and treated as some kind of input or command.

However it's not enough that a gesture is physically possible and that it's recognized by the system. Users also have to *know* that they can perform that action. There are two ways people can know: They can simply *remember* the gesture from past experience, or they can *infer* the availability of the action from some

visual indication on the screen. If the visual design signals "touch me" in those spots that are touchable, users are much more likely to know that they can touch there.

Relying on users to remember their choices is a sure prescription for poor usability. The human brain is simply not very good at remembering lots of abstract details.

When people can see what they can do, we sometimes use the term "perceived affordance" to emphasize that the action is not just doable, but also visible in advance.

Our colleague Don Norman has written much more about affordances in his classic book *The Design of Everyday Things* (Doubleday Business, 1990), which we recommend if you're interested in this topic. As Don has pointed out, most analysts don't bother distinguishing between possible affordances and perceived affordances. To be honest, we usually don't do so in this book. When we refer to "affordance," we basically mean that users can see what they can do. In other words, we're talking about perceived affordances.

The gestures that most people use naturally on the iPad are tapping and dragging. Swiping through pages seems to be easily discovered in a display that has a good horizontal scrolling affordance. But even other single-finger gestures, such as double tapping or touching and holding, are less familiar.

Once we enter the realm of multifinger gestures, the complexity increases and the likelihood of getting the gesture wrong is greater. Pinching in and out, commonly used for zooming in and out, are fairly well known, but scrolling upwards with two fingers or even the three-finger tap/drag that can be used to zoom into the page and, respectively, move around while zoomed (these gestures are defined by Apple in the Settings app of the iPad to increase accessibility) are difficult for users. We've seen several people struggling to replicate those gestures and getting them wrong.

Memory for gestures is not great, either: If your app defines new gestures that people don't normally see in other apps, the chance of them remembering those unique gestures is very small. The same rule that we know from the Web applies here: Users spend 99 percent of their time in other apps.

Recognition-based User Interfaces

Gestures are recognition-based user interfaces. This is a class of interaction design that also includes handwriting recognition, speech recognition, and natural language understanding. Common for all these interaction designs is that the computer has to interpret the raw input and try to determine what the user really means. In contrast, when the user clicks the "Buy" button on an e-commerce site or presses the "A" key on a keyboard, those actions are uniquely defined. It doesn't matter how hard or gently the user presses that key. An "A" is always what they'll get.

For gestures, on the other hand, the computer has to guess. Did the user mean to do a linear swipe or a circular motion? If the gestures are sufficiently different, it's not too hard to match the input with the intended gesture. That's also the reason it's easy to do speech recognition for a controlled vocabulary, as is often used by voice-response systems (when they prompt you to say "yes" or "no," for example).

All recognition-based user interfaces share the problem of misrecognized input, which is very frustrating for users.

Although computers have become much better at interpreting vague input, you must accept that accuracy will never be as good for recognition-based interactions as for precisely specified actions, such as button presses. This again means that you should not design overly elaborate sets of gestures that are too easily confused.

Even 99-percent recognition accuracy is probably not good enough. If you mistake users' actions as little as one percent of the time, the resulting system will feel unreliable and users will fear using it.

Using many gestures can confuse users: They are likely to forget what gesture they're supposed to use for what feature, and memories for different gestures often end up interfering with each other. Whereas some gestures have better affordances than others, the sheer multitude of features that can be accessed with gestures can easily overwhelm users.

To conclude this section, we recommend sticking to the few more-familiar gestures. If you must define new gestures, keep in mind that these will have low discoverability and poor memorability, and may suffer also from being too complex and accident prone. For these reasons, make sure that you build in some redundancy in the interface, and allow users to access all the features of your app even if they do not use the special gestures. In addition, use progressive disclosure to slowly expose users to gestures in the right context, and assign the most familiar gestures to the most frequent actions.

Accidental activation

Because the iPad screen is so much larger than a typical smartphone screen, people need to make ampler movements to reach different parts of the screen. As a result, there is an even more increased likelihood of an accidental touch compared to a smartphone.

When you combine the accidental activation with low discoverability and poor affordances, the resulting UX is frequently one of not knowing what happened or how to replicate a certain action to achieve the same result again. Worse yet, people cannot always revert to the previous state because not all apps provide an escape hatch like the Web's Back button.

Touchable areas are too small in many apps, as well as too close together, increasing the risk of accidentally touching the wrong one. In Notability, a note-taking app for the iPad (**Figure 5.9**), the targets at the top, as well as the side and bottom of the screen, are small and crowded: It's easy to press something you didn't mean to. Note also the instruction to use two fingers to scroll up and down the page when drawing (because the dragging or swiping up/down gesture is being used for drawing). Because using two fingers is a nonstandard, harder gesture and not particularly memorable (or discoverable), the interface also provides a roundabout: The little vertical page viewer on the right side of the page allows users to turn pages without scrolling.

Some apps include a false Back button (a breadcrumb button that looks like a Back button) on at least some of their pages. Why are these buttons not true Back buttons? To see the reason, let's remember the distinction from Chapter 3 between Back as up and Back as undo.

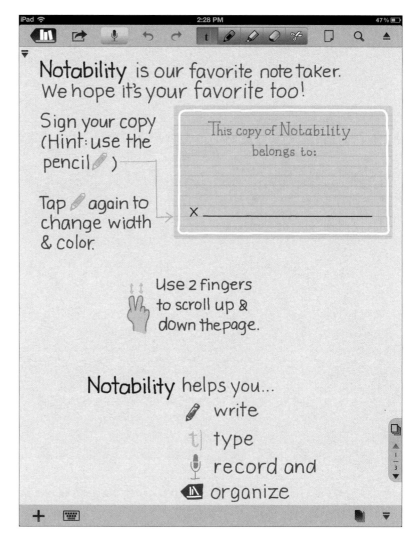

Although these breadcrumbs provide Back as up functionality, they don't work as undo, so users who accidentally tap the wrong spot on the screen often have no way of going back to the previous page.

In **Figure 5.10** you can see how Back as up can cause problems. In the Hotels.com app, users who have searched for a hotel and selected one from the search results page are taken, as expected, to the hotel page. However when they navigate one more step away from that page (by pressing the "Book now" button) and reach the pricing page, tapping the Back button takes them back to the search results page, not to the hotel page. At this point, they need to find the hotel again in the list.

Figure 5.10 Hotels.com's app for the iPad uses Back as up instead of Back as undo. (**A**) A search results page is generated in response to a user query. (**B**) The hotel page is reached from the search results page. (**C**) The pricing page is accessed by pressing "Book now" on the hotel page. Tapping the Back button on this page takes the user back to the search results, not to the hotel page.

Inconsistent Interaction Design

Once they do figure out how something works, users rarely can transfer their skills from one app to the next. Each application has a completely different UI for similar features.

In different apps (or sometimes even in the same app), touching a picture could produce any of the following several results:

- Nothing special happens (**Figure 5.11A**)

- Enlarging the picture (**Figure 5.11B**)

- Showing a more detailed page about that item (**Figure 5.11C**)

- Flipping the image to reveal additional pictures in the same place (metaphorically, these new pictures are "on the back side" of the original picture)

- Popping up a set of navigation choices

- Showing tips about interacting with the image (**Figure 5.11D**)

In the *New Yorker* magazine app (Figure 5.11A–B), tapping on an image can either trigger the same action as tapping anywhere on the

Figure 5.11 Tapping on an image can cause different reactions in different iPad apps. (**A**) In the *New Yorker* magazine app it displays the top and bottom navigation bars; (**B**) Also in the *New Yorker*, tapping on a cartoon shows an enlarged version; (**C**) In *Life*'s app, it shows action buttons as well as the title of the photograph; (**D**) The Zappos app displays some tips about interacting with the image.

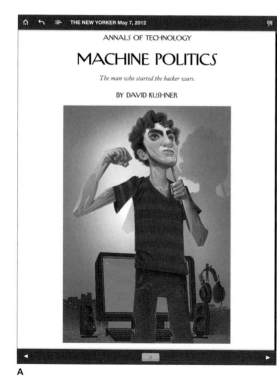

A

B

page (namely, it exposes the magazine's navigation bar at the top and slider at the bottom), or it can show an enlarged version of the same image. The lack of consistency is even more critical within the same app: Users don't necessarily expect different effects to be associated with the same action.

In the *USA Today* app, the newspaper's logo brought up a navigation menu listing the various sections (**Figure 5.12**). This was probably the most unexpected interaction we tested, and not one user discovered it in our initial test back in 2010.

We went back to the *USA Today* app and tested it a year later in 2011. Even a year after the iPad's release, users with substantial tablet experience still couldn't use this design. One of our test users was a regular user of this app. Although he said he had eventually discovered the section navigation on his own, during the test session he complained bitterly about how difficult it had been to find. Users rarely remember the details of interaction design widgets, which is one of the key reasons that it's better to watch users than to ask them about usability. The fact that this user recalled his troubles months later is a testament to how strikingly annoying the old navigation design was.

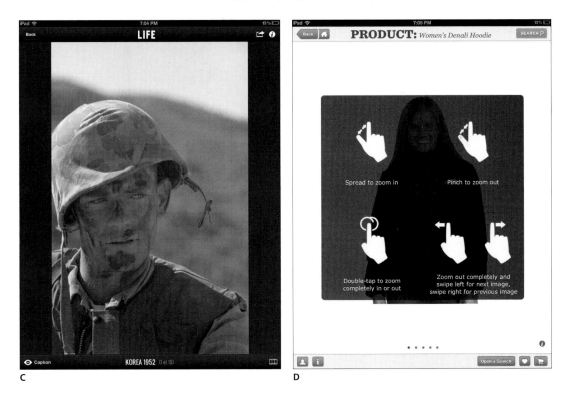

C

D

Figure 5.12 *USA Today's* initial iPad app design.

Fortunately, a few days after our last test sessions, *USA Today* released a new version of its app with somewhat improved navigation (**Figure 5.13**). To bring up the section menu, the user now has to touch an explicitly named Sections button. This is a dramatically better design than the newspaper's previous app shown in Figure 5.12.

We see a similar lack of consistency when it comes to within–article navigation. To continue reading once you reach the bottom of the screen might require any of three different gestures:

- Scrolling down within a text field while staying within the same page.

  For this gesture to work, you have to touch within the text field. However text fields aren't demarcated on the screen, so you have to guess what text is scrollable.

- Swiping left (which can sometimes take you to the next article instead of showing more of the current article).

  This gesture doesn't work if you happen to swipe within an area covered by an advertisement or by a carousel (see also our discussion in the section "Swipe Ambiguity" later in this chapter).

- Swiping up.

Figure 5.13 *USA Today's* revised iPad app. The Sections button in the upper-left corner exposes the navigation.

In the *Popular Science* magazine app (**Figure 5.14**), scrolling is done sometimes by swiping vertically within a text box and sometimes by scrolling anywhere on the page. On some pages, as the text scrolls, an existing image appears in the background of new text, making it more difficult to read. Swiping left takes users to the next article. Note also the practice of fitting the text in a narrow column, giving a lot of extra space to the picture. This is an attempt to cater to users' fascination with beautiful pictures on the iPad. But unfortunately it is a poor use of the screen, because it increases the amount of scrolling and the memory overload and, ultimately, makes the article harder to read.

A

B

Figure 5.14 Several *types* of scrolling in the *Popular Science* magazine app. (**A**) Vertical scrolling is done in the text box. (**B**) Scrolling works by swiping anywhere on the page. (**C**) As the user scrolls down, new text appears on top of the helicopters in Figure 5.14B.

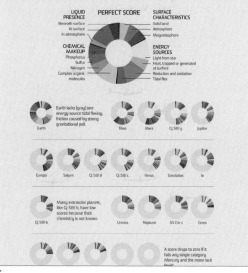

C

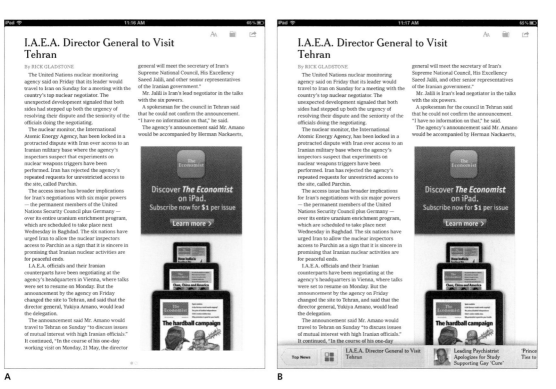

Figure 5.15 Scrolling in the *New York Times* app for iPad. (**A**) Horizontal scrolling (swiping) moves to the next page in the article. (**B**) When the navigation bar at the bottom is exposed, swiping must be done outside it to navigate to the next page.

In the *New York Times* app (**Figure 5.15**), horizontal scrolling (swiping) leads to the next page in the article or (on the last page) to the next article. However when the navigation bar at the bottom is exposed, swiping must be done outside it to navigate to the next page. (Swiping within the navigation bar shows other article titles.)

Over time we have seen some progress in the consistency of design. Users aren't as tormented by widely diverging UIs, and apps have become more consistent and standardized. However, as these examples point out, there's still unpredictability, sometimes within the same app.

The Print Metaphor

Swiping for the next article is derived from a strong print metaphor in many content apps. In fact, when the first iPad apps came out, this metaphor was so strong that you couldn't even tap a headline on the "cover" page to jump to the corresponding article. Although most apps no longer have that issue, some—like *Popular Science* magazine (**Figure 5.16**)—still perseverate.

Figure 5.16 The *Popular Science* cover contains no hyperlinks. None of the headlines on the cover are tappable.

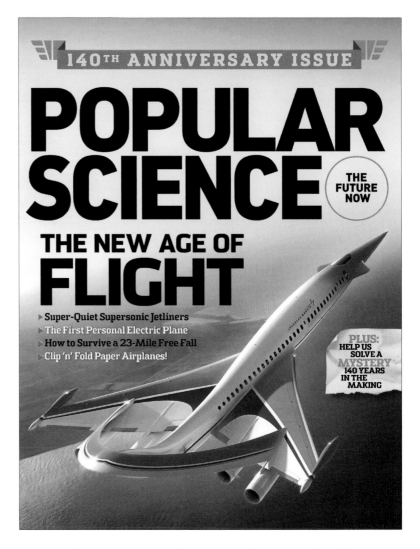

Sequential navigation is another practice that comes from the print era and makes little sense in electronic media. In digital contexts, the linear concept of "next article" is often artificial and restrictive. People would rather choose where to go, selecting from a menu of related offerings.

A strategic issue for iPad user experience design is whether to emphasize user empowerment or author authority. Some designs err on the side of being too limiting in their allegiance to the print metaphor. Using the Web has given people an appreciation for freedom and control, and they're unlikely to happily revert to a linear experience.

Publishers hope that users will perceive content as more valuable if each publication is a stand-alone environment. Similarly, they hope for higher value-added if users spend more time with fewer publications rather than flit among a huge range of sites like they do on the Web.

Using the desktop Web, a user can easily visit 100 sites in a week, viewing only one to three pages on most of them. (For example, in one study we observed a user who visited 15 sites to buy a single product. The sites were distributed across search engines, review sites, vendor sites, and retailer sites. Only one site got the sale, of course.) Most sites are visited only once, because users dredge them up in a search or stumble upon links from other sites or social media postings. Without real customer relationships, content sites have no value and 90 percent of the money created by users spending time online accrues to search engines.

The current design strategy of iPad apps definitely aims to create more immersive experiences in the hope of inspiring deeper attachments to individual information sources. This cuts against the lesson of the Web, where diversity is strength and no site can hope to capture users' sole attention. Frequent user movement among websites has driven the imperative to conform to interface conventions and to create designs that people can use without any learning (or even much looking around). The iPad is different because, whether people do have a lot of apps on their device or not, they end up sticking with just a few of them that they use on a regular basis.

Card Sharks vs. Holy Scrollers

UI pioneer Jef Raskin once used the phrase "*card sharks vs. holy scrollers*" to distinguish between two fundamentally different hypertext models:

- Cards have a fixed-size presentation canvas. You can position your information within this two-dimensional space to your heart's content (allowing for beautiful layouts), but you can't make it any bigger. Users have to jump to a new card to get more info than will fit on a single card. HyperCard was the most famous example of this model.

- Scrolls provide room for as much information as you want because the canvas can extend as far down as you please. Users have to jump less, but at the cost of a less-fancy layout because the designer can't control what users are seeing at any given time.

The Web is firmly in the holy-scroller camp, particularly these days: Users scroll a fair amount and sometimes view information far down long pages. Even mobile-phone apps often rely on scrolling to present more than will fit on their tiny screens.

In contrast, card sharks tend to dominate the iPad designs. Although some apps mix the two models or remain faithful to the Web model, many apps try to create a fixed layout for the pretty screen.

The card model works better in certain types of apps—especially news and magazine apps. There, the print metaphor is strong enough to make the swipe gesture relatively discoverable (it's still not the first gesture that users will try, but they eventually discover it). In other contexts (such as the cocktail recipe app in **Figure 5.17**), however, the card model is harder to discover and may have benefited from some cues for horizontal navigation.

Indeed, even for those apps for which the card model is less natural, there are easy ways of making the swipe gesture more discoverable. Most of them involve showing some visible cues indicating the direction of navigation: Arrows (**Figure 5.18A**) or visibly truncated content that creates the illusion of continuity (**Figure 5.18B**) are usually strong hints, whereas dots at the bottom of a page or an image tend to work less well (**Figure 5.18C**), simply because they are less noticeable and blend more with the background.

Figure 5.17 In Martha Stewart's Cocktails for iPad, the deck of cards navigation model that requires users to swipe to the left for the next recipe is less discoverable.

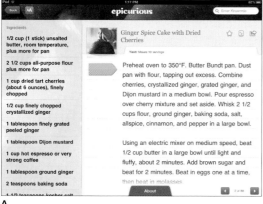

A

B

Figure 5.18 Cues that increase the discoverability of the horizontal swipe: (**A**) Epicurious uses arrows in the bottom-right corner. (**B**) Marvel shows a small fragment of the next or previous page on the sides of the screen. (**C**) The Weather Channel shows dots to indicate multiple screens in the top panel and the illusion of continuity in the two other panels.

C

Whether you use vertical or horizontal scrolling in your app, stay faithful to one method of navigation and don't mix the two—either on the same page or in different orientations. Amazon Windowshop uses both horizontal and vertical scrolling on the same page (**Figure 5.19**). The app displays a big table of products with different columns representing different product categories. You can swipe horizontally to see more product categories, and you can swipe vertically to see more items within the displayed categories. A product can be displayed under multiple categories (for instance, an iPad appears in Computers & Accessories, Kindle Store, Apple Store, and Electronics). When we tested this app, users couldn't remember which items they had seen before and were completely disoriented.

Time magazine (**Figure 5.20**) uses (mostly) horizontal swiping in the landscape orientation but mixes horizontal and vertical scrolling in portrait. Within the same app, you can read the next page of an article either by swiping or by scrolling vertically. *Time* does cue the users to scroll vertically by using small arrows and the words "Scroll to read more" in red. However our participants were surprised and had a hard time adjusting to the different navigation methods in the two orientations: Users shouldn't have to learn a new interface when they change from portrait to landscape or vice versa.

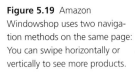

Figure 5.19 Amazon Windowshop uses two navigation methods on the same page: You can swipe horizontally or vertically to see more products.

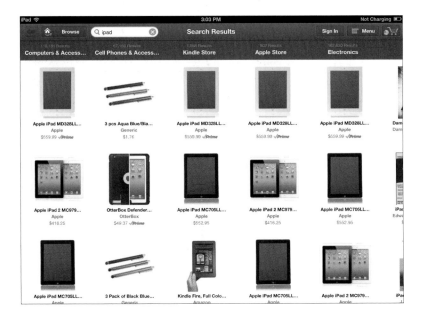

Figure 5.20 The *Time* magazine app uses different navigation schemes on different pages of the app. Within the same app, you can read the next page of an article either by (**A**) swiping or (**B**) scrolling vertically.

A

B

Swipe Ambiguity

One problem with using the swipe gesture to move back and forth is that it can interfere with other elements on the page that require horizontal navigation and especially with carousels (**Figure 5.21**). We call this overloading of the swipe gesture *swipe ambiguity* (see also our discussion in the section "Overloaded vs. Generic Commands" in Chapter 3). Most of the time when users flip the page, they do not position their finger consistently in a particular spot on the page (such as the lower-right corner); instead they tend to do it as if they are using a physical book. If there are any spots on the page where the swipe gesture does not work, the user will perceive the application as erratic.

Figure 5.21 Swipe ambiguity in *Time* magazine: (**A**) An article page contains a carousel in the lower half of the screen. (**B**) Swiping horizontally in the bottom half of the page moves the book carousel rather than turning the page.

A page from the *Time* magazine app shows the swipe ambiguity in action: Because the bottom half of the page (Figure 5.21A) is occupied by a carousel, swiping horizontally takes users to the next article if the gesture is localized in the top half of the screen but moves the carousel in the bottom half of the screen (Figure 5.21B). Users often don't think about localizing the swipe, especially when the swipe has tended to work anywhere on the page in the past. A big carousel on the page can interfere with the regular swiping.

Does that mean that the swipe gesture is doomed and that you should simply stay away from it? No, it just means that you have to take into account the fact that users won't necessarily hit a specific spot. (If you want them to hit a specific spot, you're better off providing a button). What we do know about swiping gestures is that typically they are executed close to the sides of the screen (although where on the sides we cannot tell), in the same way in which people turn the pages of a book. That means that leaving some margin of safe, noninterfering space (not necessarily white space, just not a carousel) around the vertical edges of the screen will be good enough in most situations. Not covering the page with carousels is another solution: If the carousel occupies only a small proportion of the page, the chance that a user will hit it when swiping will decrease.

TMN: Too Much Navigation

Many apps squeeze information into very small areas, making it harder to recognize and manipulate. In a related problem, some apps feature too much navigation. This design problem is so prevalent that it deserves its own acronym: TMN. Although it's true that there are at least 25 different navigation techniques to choose from (counting by the number we cover in our IA courses), any given user interface should contain only a few. These two problems interact because a larger number of navigation options gives each one less space.

ATT U-verse is a case of TMN (**Figure 5.22**). The app uses two different methods of navigation. The first method of navigation is the traditional grid that shows what's on at a given time on several channels. Users can scroll horizontally or vertically to see more. Although the double scrolling is less than ideal, this type of data visualization is what most users expect and are familiar with from paper TV guides. The second method of navigation is the carousel that showcases one channel and one program at a time. Users need to scroll painfully through the thousands of channels available and see what's on right now. The experience is similar to zapping through the channels with a remote control, but the actual program is replaced with a description of the program. Our research shows that users rarely have the patience to swipe through a carousel for a long list: The process is just too slow and inefficient. As one of our users put it, *"I don't know what the twentieth item in this list is, but I know that I will never find out."*

Figure 5.22 ATT U-verse for the iPad provides two different methods of navigation: (**A**) a grid showing programs and channels and (**B**) a carousel displaying one channel and one program at a time.

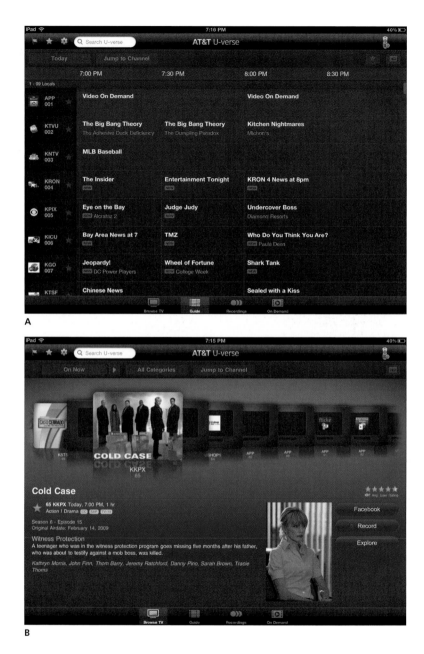

A

B

One example of excess navigation involves the displaying of thumbnails of available articles or items. In magazine apps, sometimes these thumbnails are accessed by scrubbing a slider (**Figure 5.23A–B**), and sometimes they appear in table-of-contents popovers (**Figure 5.23C**) or carousels. Unfortunately, none of these is an efficient method of navigation. The tap-and-hold scrubber is not very discoverable, and people

A

B

C

Figure 5.23 *Vanity Fair* provides several ways to navigate to an article: (**A**) An article carousel with thumbnails of entire articles; (**B**) A scrubber that shows the thumbnail and title of the article when tapped and held; (**C**) A table of contents split view that displays a tiny thumbnail and the article title; (**D**) A hyperlinked version of the table of contents page in the magazine.

D

don't like its nondeterministic nature (depending on the dragging speed, they may miss certain articles). The spread-out page carousel is good *"if you are at a red light"* (as one of our participants put it) and want to pick a short article, but it still requires a fair amount of scrolling to find an article. The table of contents popover (or split view) shows too small thumbnails and text, and still needs quite a lot of horizontal scrolling. Whatever the implementation, these long lists of thumbnails have lower usability than homepage-like tables of contents (**Figure 5.23D**) to which users can return when they want to navigate to different locations rather than simply continuing with the next article. (In fact, many of our users who were looking for a particular article just selected the Table of Contents article in the table of contents popover instead of searching for the article inside the popover.)

Another example from a recent study comes courtesy of NASA (**Figure 5.24**). The main screen on NASA's iPad app is a visualization of the solar system. This is not a highly efficient use of space, but it's actually OK because it's an engaging image that offers a wide selection of choices from the opening screen while clearly communicating what the app is all about.

Figure 5.24 NASA's iPad app: The home screen with the drop-down menu expanded.

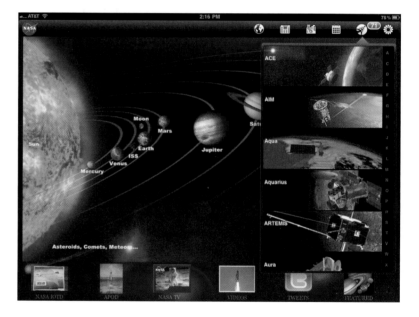

In user testing, the main problem with this screen was the risk of touching the wrong heavenly body: The distance between the earth and the moon is only 60 percent of the usability guideline for separating objects in touch-screen applications. Touchable items should be at least one centimeter across (0.4 inches).

Another usability problem is related to space utilization (screen space, not outer space). The drop-down menu featuring satellite missions was difficult to use for two reasons. First, the button's icon looked more like a fish skeleton than a satellite, but that was a relatively minor issue.

Second, the bigger problem was that it was *physically hard to move* through the long list of missions—doing so seemed to require almost infinite scrolling. Also, each satellite was *hard to recognize* from its picture and acronym. Most satellites look much the same unless you're even more of a space nerd than NASA has the right to expect of its users.

The designers tried to emulate a mega menu but failed to achieve its benefits for several reasons:

- **There's no categorization of the menu items.** A good mega menu would have broken the missions into groups and given each group a title. Doing so would make it much easier to find certain types of satellites, such as those for inner-planet exploration.

- **Labels are not explained.** For example, it might be helpful to know that "ACE" measures high-energy particles, whereas "AIM" studies mesosphere ice.

- **Illustrations are meaningless.** Pretty fluff, but still fluff.

Instead of the ever-scrolling menu, it would have been better to take users to a separate full-screen overview that showed all the missions in a single view, making them much easier to compare. Spending more screen space is OK as long as you give users an easy way back to the main view.

The proliferation of small, hard-to-use interaction areas in iPad apps is partly Apple's fault because of an uninspired design in the default email application (**Figure 5.25**). The inbox is shown as a skinny menu down the side. This is great in landscape view because it lets users quickly alternate between the inbox and individual messages so they can rapidly process their mail. In portrait orientation, however, the inbox menu appears as an overlay that partly obscures the message content, making it impossible to work with the two panes simultaneously. Why show two panes when you can't use both? To optimize reading, it would be better to display the inbox across the entire tablet screen, showing more messages and/or more extensive previews of each message. Instead, the designers chose to optimize for saving state rather than for using screen space: It makes it easy for users who, say, were reading an email message to quickly check their mailbox by tapping the button at the top, getting the content of the inbox in a popover, dismissing the popover, and going back to the message they were reading.

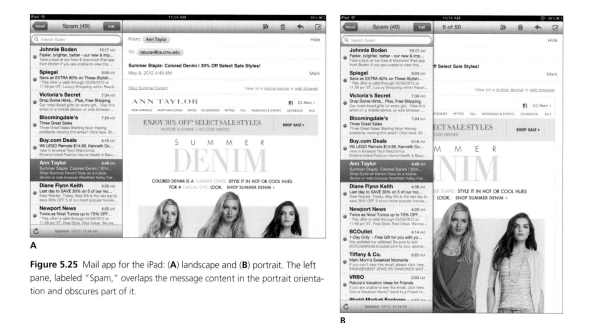

Figure 5.25 Mail app for the iPad: (**A**) landscape and (**B**) portrait. The left pane, labeled "Spam," overlaps the message content in the portrait orientation and obscures part of it.

Although popovers and split views (as in the Mail app shown in Figure 5.25) were initially intended for the bigger iPad screen, they've started to proliferate on the iPhone as well (**Figure 5.26**). Unfortunately on the iPhone they utilize just a small fraction of the already small screen and force users to scroll in a tiny dialog, which is unproductive most of the time. In addition, the content in the popover often gets truncated (Figure 5.26A) or displayed in a smaller font that can be difficult to read for anybody over 40. (Many mobile designers may be in their 30s, but trust us, your eyesight will start to decay soon enough.)

One of the attractions of popovers or split views is that they preserve context: Users can continue to see ("in the background" or on the side) the page they were on before the popover appeared. This benefit disappears on the iPhone because the screen is so tiny: Whatever is visible from the old page will be useless when a popover covers or displaces most of it.

Note also that, unlike for the iPad's Mail app (Figure 5.25), allowing users to quickly check for new content and then return to whatever they were doing before doesn't really count as a benefit when popovers are used as static menus (as in the examples in Figure 5.26), because the information in the popover never changes: Users don't normally check the list of topics or genres and go back to their list of articles or channels (unless they tap that popover accidentally; a Back button should take care of that case anyway).

Figure 5.26 Split views and popovers on the iPhone: (**A**) sliding split view in AP Mobile and (**B**) popover in U-verse.

Splash Screens and Startup Noises

Splash screens are another ancient Web practice that has suffered a revival in the iPad era. We thought we had driven a stake through splash screens many years ago with Jakob Nielsen's early book *Designing Web Usability* (Peachpit Press, 1999). But apparently splash screens are super vampires that can haunt users from beyond the grave. Several new iPad apps have long introductory segments that might be entertaining the first time but soon wear out their welcome—bad on sites and bad in apps, so don't use them.

Re-baptized as launch screens, splash screens often contain no information about how long the app is going to take to load and no progress bar, and in addition have no relationship whatsoever to the first screen of the app.

Many designers feel compelled to start their apps with elaborate graphics. Sometimes complex animations that can take quite a few seconds are involved. Whereas a cute animation can bring a smile the first time the app is started, by the fifth time it becomes annoying.

Some apps take a step beyond and add video or noises to the splash screen. Apps such as Martha Stewart Cocktails and Al Gore's Our Choice also start by playing a video. Others, such as Moviefone and Gilt, make a noise when the app is started. We strongly advise against startup sounds. Users do not expect to hear noises when they start an app (and often they may do it in circumstances where noises are inappropriate—imagine suddenly hearing "*Welcome to Moviefone*" in the middle of a staff meeting).

Orientation

Participants in our studies were told in the beginning that they could use whatever iPad orientation was most comfortable to them and could switch orientations as they saw fit. Most of the time, our participants picked an orientation at the beginning of the session and used it for the entire session. They rarely switched orientations spontaneously, and when they did so, it was because they thought they would get a better look at a picture, see the text in a larger font, or watch a video full screen. Sometimes the application forced them to work in a different orientation.

Slightly more users mentioned that they preferred the landscape orientation for the iPad. A seemingly related factor was whether they were using an iPad cover; those who did mentioned that they often propped up their iPad in landscape orientation. Also, computer monitors are typically in landscape orientation, as one user explained:

"My computer screen at work and my laptop screen at home are landscape. Intuitively, when I am looking at an electronic screen, my mind tells me to look at it in landscape mode. I try to play around with landscape versus portrait in the context of photos. [For] anything like reading or viewing a video, I automatically switch to landscape mode."

Many apps strive to take advantage of the extra horizontal space available in the landscape view. Unfortunately in some cases they push it too far: Certain features of the app are not available unless the user changes the orientation of the device.

In the case of the BBC app (**Figure 5.27**), we witnessed several users having trouble finding the health or the sports section: Unfortunately those topics were accessible only in landscape mode. BBC also changes the layout of the page in landscape by morphing the top within-page navigation bar into a navigation panel. None of our users seemed to be aware that the app may behave differently in a different orientation: The discoverability of those features available in a single different orientation is extremely low.

Because we cannot predict how users will hold the device, we recommend that all functionalities be accessible in all orientations, even if the layout may vary somewhat from portrait to landscape. We also

The Microsoft Surface tablets feature a built-in kickstand that encourages use of the device in landscape mode. At the time of this writing, we had not yet tested any Surface users, but we would expect landscape use to be somewhat more prevalent on this device because of the orientation bias provided by the kickstand.

recommend that the app be as consistent as possible: If a navigation popover is displayed to the left in portrait, don't move it to the right in landscape or vice versa (**Figure 5.28**).

Figure 5.27 BBC app for iPad displays different content in the two orientations: (**A**) landscape and (**B**) portrait.

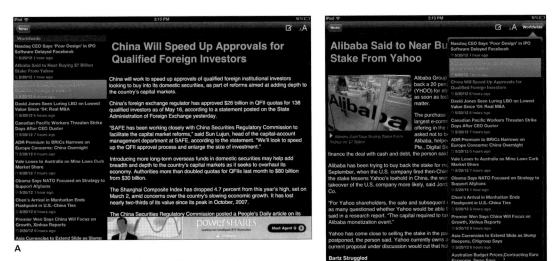

Figure 5.28 Bloomberg for iPad in two different orientations: (**A**) landscape and (**B**) portrait. The left-side navigation panel in landscape view gets transformed into a popover and moved to the right in portrait view.

Toward a Better iPad User Experience

It's nice to see that iPad user interfaces have become decidedly less wacky than they were right after the release of the tablet. It's even better to see good uptake of several of our early recommendations, including apps with:

- Back buttons

- Broader use of search

- Homepages

- Direct access to articles by touching headlines on the front page

Even so, our newer testing still found many cases in which users accidentally touched something and couldn't find their way back to their start point, as well as magazine apps that required multiple steps to access the table of contents.

To make iPad designs more usable:

- Add dimensionality and better define individual interactive areas to increase discoverability through perceived affordances of what users can do where.

- To achieve these interactive benefits, loosen up the etched-glass aesthetic. Going beyond the flatland of iPad's first-generation apps might create slightly less-attractive screens, but designers can retain most of the good looks by making the GUI cues more subtle than the heavy-handed visuals used in the Macintosh-to-Windows-7 progression of GUI styles.

- Abandon the hope of value-added through weirdness. It's better to use consistent interaction techniques that empower users to focus on your content instead of wondering how to get it.

- Support standard navigation, including a Back feature, search, clickable headlines, and a homepage for most apps.

Kindle Usability

Amazon sells several Kindle devices: Although most are primarily marketed and used as e-readers, Kindle Fire is a midsize tablet in its own right. In this section we talk first about the older versions of Kindle that use electronic ink and function primarily as e-readers, and then we discuss the usability of Kindle Fire as the most popular midsize tablet.

Kindle: The E-reader

Kindle shines in one area of interaction design: turning the page. This *one command* has *two buttons* (on either side of the device). Paging backwards is a less-common action, nicely supported with a separate, smaller button.

Thus the device offers good support for the task of linear reading—appropriately so, because Kindle's design is centered on this one use case. While reading, your only interaction is to repeatedly press the next-page button.

Anything else is awkward.

In the first-generation Kindle, most Kindle interactions were mediated by a small joystick called *the 5-way*, which let you move the cursor in four directions; pressing down enabled the fifth action. Newer versions of Kindle have replaced the 5-way with five equivalent buttons: four arrow buttons and a center button. Moving the cursor around the screen is extremely tedious, whether you're using a 5-way or arrow buttons. It doesn't feel like direct manipulation at all. Getting the cursor where you want it requires a lot of work.

Also, the Kindle is slow. Every time you enter a command, it ponders the situation before acting. Even turning the page takes slightly longer than it should, and all other actions are definitely sluggish.

In short, awkward pointing + slow reaction = a bad UX that discourages people from exploring and attempting different tasks.

Poor design for nonlinear content

The usability problem with nonlinear content is crucial because it indicates a deeper issue: Kindle's UX is dominated by the book metaphor. The idea that you'd want to start on a section's first page makes sense for a book because most are based on linear exposition. Unfortunately this is untrue for many other content collections, including newspapers, magazines, and even some nonfiction books, such as travel guides, encyclopedias, and cookbooks.

So the design decisions that make the Kindle good for reading novels (and linear nonfiction) make it a suboptimal device for reading nonlinear content. Sure, Amazon designers could fix simple UI stupidities, such as the interaction design for a newspaper table of contents. But doing so would simply apply a Band-Aid. To truly optimize the nonlinear user experience, they'd have to completely reconceptualize the Kindle design.

Amazon also provides an iPhone application that can display Kindle-format e-books (**Figure 5.29A**). It does take slightly more time to read a book with the iPhone than with a Kindle because of the time spent turning pages on the smaller device.

When using our preferred font sizes, reading on the Kindle iPhone app required 21 percent more page turns than reading on a Kindle. With the iPhone application's default font size — which we find a bit too big—the iPhone app requires 100 percent more page turns than the Kindle.

The Kindle iPhone app displays pages with fully justified text (that is, flush left and right). This reduces legibility slightly, particularly for the small telephone screen's narrow columns. iBooks (Apple's book reader app) uses left-justified text only, which is a better choice (**Figure 5.29B**) for reading, because the eye does not need to adjust to the various width of white space between words. Kindle's default font is a little too big, whereas the iBooks' manages to show more text on the page (as well as a title and page count) while still preserving legibility.

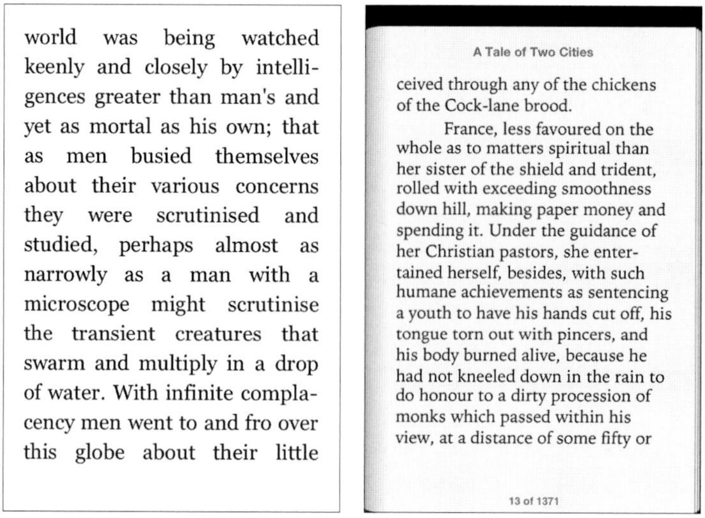

Figure 5.29 Book reading apps on the iPhone: (**A**) Kindle and (**B**) iBooks. The Kindle displays the text fully justified, whereas iBooks uses left-justified text.

world was being watched keenly and closely by intelligences greater than man's and yet as mortal as his own; that as men busied themselves about their various concerns they were scrutinised and studied, perhaps almost as narrowly as a man with a microscope might scrutinise the transient creatures that swarm and multiply in a drop of water. With infinite complacency men went to and fro over this globe about their little

A Tale of Two Cities

ceived through any of the chickens of the Cock-lane brood.

France, less favoured on the whole as to matters spiritual than her sister of the shield and trident, rolled with exceeding smoothness down hill, making paper money and spending it. Under the guidance of her Christian pastors, she entertained herself, besides, with such humane achievements as sentencing a youth to have his hands cut off, his tongue torn out with pincers, and his body burned alive, because he had not kneeled down in the rain to do honour to a dirty procession of monks which passed within his view, at a distance of some fifty or

13 of 1371

A   B

Cross-device integration

The Kindle iPhone app has poor usability but shines in its integration with other Kindle apps and devices. This is one of the first good examples of supporting multiple computers and using wireless connectivity to do so.

You can buy a book on the website using your desktop computer and its superior browsing usability. You can then read the book on the Kindle at home, on your smartphone in the dentist's waiting room, or even on your iPad on a plane ride. In fact you can alternate between reading the same book on different devices: They'll automatically coordinate so that you pick up the book on one screen in the same position where you left it on the other screen.

Much has been made of a user's ability to buy books directly on the Kindle. However buying books on a full-featured PC with the full Amazon.com site is much easier.

Still, Amazon deserves praise for the smooth integration between buying on the PC and reading your purchase on the Kindle. Assuming you're in one of the supported countries and have wireless coverage, all it takes is one click on the PC, and the book shows up on your Kindle without any special installation.

Electronic books: good or bad idea?

The Pew Internet report is called "The rise of e-reading" (Pew Internet, 2012) by L. Rainie, K. Zickuhr, K. Purcell, M. Madden, and J. Brenner. It is available for download at http:// libraries.pewinternet.org/2012/04/04/ the-rise-of-e-reading.

In 1998 Jakob Nielsen wrote an essay titled "Electronic Books— A Bad Idea." Today we would say that they are a good idea, at least for fiction and simpler nonfiction. By February 2012, according to statistics from Pew Internet, over a fifth of Americans had read an e-book, and approximately 30 percent of them owned a device such as a tablet or e-reader that allowed them to read e-books.

What happened? Amazon's aggressive pricing strategy for e-books has probably played an important role. But from a usability perspective, three essential factors were a) convenience, b) equal-to-print readability, and c) multidevice integration.

There's some benefit to having an information appliance specialized for reading fiction and linear nonfiction books that don't depend on illustrations or require readers to refer back and forth between sections.

For people who travel or commute using public transportation, e-books can be useful for a few reasons:

- There's less weight to schlep around (carrying ten books on one device would have been particularly nice during a recent trip around the Serengeti where we were allowed only 22 pounds of luggage for a two-week safari).
- No dirty fingers from newsprint.
- It's easier to turn pages while riding a crowded train or bus.

Being able to sync with a phone or iPad extends the usefulness scenarios. If you're waiting in the doctor's office, for example, and don't have your e-reader, you can pull out your phone and make use of otherwise wasted time. Multidevice reading is one area where the Kindle is better than reality: It does something a printed book can't do.

In addition to travelers and commuters, a second favored user group includes elderly people and those with reduced vision. Big fonts, together with multidevice reading, are Kindle's two better-than-reality features.

However, for people who just read books at home, print will do just fine. For linear reading the Kindle offers no advantages, but for non-linear content it has many disadvantages.

Kindle Fire Usability

Amazon.com's Kindle Fire offers a disappointingly poor user experience. Using the Web with the Silk browser is clunky and error prone. Reading downloaded magazines is not much better. Still, user testing with the Fire did help us understand whether the new generation of 7-inch tablets is more like a 10-inch tablet (such as the iPad) or more like a 3.5-inch mobile phone. To give away the conclusion, the answer is "a bit of both."

The "fat finger" problem makes mobile sites superior

The most striking observation from testing the Fire is that everything is much too small on the screen, leading to frequent tap errors and accidental activation. You haven't seen the fat finger problem in its full glory until you've watched users struggle to touch targets on the Fire. One poor guy spent several minutes trying to log in to Facebook but was repeatedly foiled by accidentally touching the wrong field or button—this on a page with only two text fields and one button (**Figure 5.30**). (Since we tested this app, Facebook has slightly changed its login page—not necessarily for the better, as shown in **Figure 5.31**).

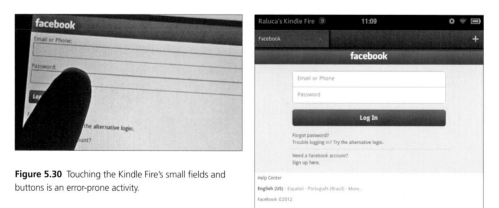

Figure 5.30 Touching the Kindle Fire's small fields and buttons is an error-prone activity.

Figure 5.31 The newer login page on Facebook.com: The fields are still crowded, and the Login button is dangerously close to the "Forgot password?" link.

At the beginning of this chapter, we said that full sites work quite well on 10-inch tablets. And, as discussed in Chapter 2, testing mobile phones revealed that specialized mobile sites are superior on phone-size touch screens (typically, 3- to 5-inch diagonal).

Using desktop designs on a 7-inch tablet is like squeezing a size-10 person into a size-6 suit: It's not going to look good. But that's what the Fire is trying to do. Accessing desktop sites on the Fire was a prescription for failure in our testing. The Kindle Fire's screen is too small for reading text on a normal desktop page without zooming in. Users did much better when using mobile sites (**Figure 5.32**); thus, the Kindle Fire is closer to a large-screen phone than to a large-screen tablet.

Using sites optimized for 3.5-inch mobile screens on the bigger 7-inch screen felt luxurious—somewhat like using a regular website on a 30-inch monitor. You have all the space in the world and can see the entire page with little (if any) scrolling.

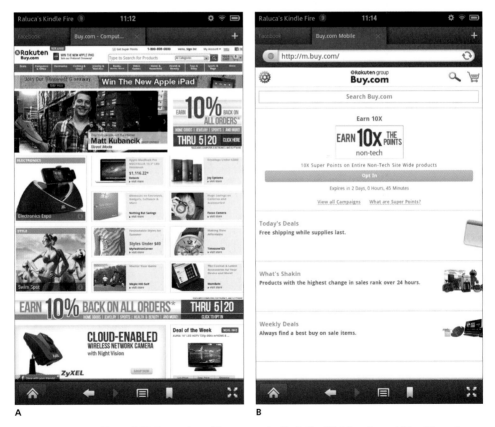

Figure 5.32 Two versions of Buy.com on the Kindle Fire: (**A**) full version and (**B**) mobile version. Mobile sites work better on the Fire.

Using the Kindle Fire

Our studies of the Kindle Fire weren't intended to advise consumers on whether to buy a Fire device. Our goal was to discover design guidelines for companies that are building websites, apps, or content that *their* customers might access on a Fire.

Even so, we have some observations on the physical device based on our personal use and on the usability study.

The Fire is a heavy object. It's unpleasant to hold for extended periods of time. Unless you have forearm muscles like Popeye, you can't comfortably sit and read an engaging novel all evening. The lack of physical buttons for turning the page also impedes on the reading experience for fiction. On the older Kindles, it's easy to keep a finger on the button when all you use it for is to turn the page. In contrast, tapping an area of the screen disrupts reading enjoyment, is slightly error prone, and leaves smudges on the screen. The Fire screen also has more glare than the traditional Kindle.

For reading fiction, the regular Kindle device wins.

For nonfiction, such as textbooks and magazines, the regular Kindle's awkward interaction design precludes easy navigation, and the grayscale screen doesn't display illustrations properly.

Compared to the regular Kindle, the Kindle Fire could win big for reading magazines and other light nonfiction, provided that magazine apps learn from their counterparts on the iPad. Deeper reading that requires users to frequently refer to other parts of the text is still not well supported. Even with a touch screen, within-book navigation is slow and awkward, so we don't recommend the Kindle Fire for reading textbooks.

Most of the time, however, the magazine reading experience is actually miserable because the content isn't designed for the device or for interactive reading.

Many of the magazine apps designed for the Kindle Fire resemble the first iPad magazine apps (**Figure 5.33**): They are essentially just magazine spreads (scanned versions of the physical magazine). The magazine spread (namely, the so-called *Page view*—Figure 5.33A) didn't work on the iPad and does not work on the Fire: The screen is simply too small for people to be able to read the text. Hence the invention of the so-called *Text view* (Figure 5.33B), which is a dump of the article text with one or two illustrations placed throughout and very basic formatting.

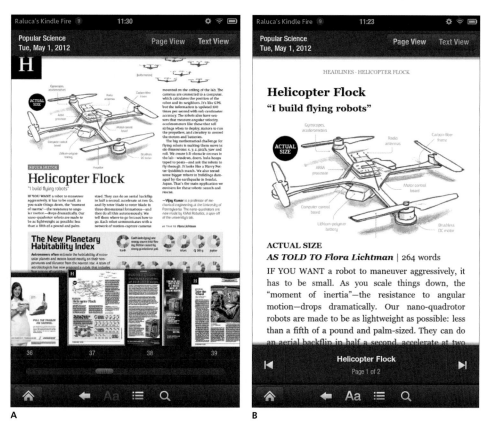

Figure 5.33 *Popular Science* for the Kindle Fire: (**A**) Page view and (**B**) Text view.

In this type of magazine, the navigation is done only through horizontal swiping, and there are no hyperlinks—only sequential access to an article. Gone is the excess navigation from the iPad magazines: The scrubber at the bottom of the page is the only way to browse quickly through the magazine.

Vanity Fair for the Kindle Fire (**Figure 5.34**) takes a completely different approach than *Popular Science*. The app has exactly the same interface as the iPad, complete with hyperlinks and the three different navigation methods: table-of-contents pane, carousel page viewer, and page scrubber at the bottom. This interface is superior to the *Popular Science* one, simply because it offers a richer experience (not because of the excess navigation, but because of the hyperlinking). The text in the table-of-contents pane is so tiny that it serves just to help users find the actual table-of-contents page in the magazine and use that as a navigation hub. Note also that the app has claimed the space used for the Kindle's virtual buttons, and the user needs to navigate to the app's home (top-left corner) to recover them.

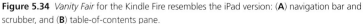

A B

Figure 5.34 *Vanity Fair* for the Kindle Fire resembles the iPad version: (**A**) navigation bar and scrubber, and (**B**) table-of-contents pane.

Here's a summary of the main sins of magazine apps on the Kindle Fire:

- Many magazines don't have a "homepage" to which users can return after finishing an article.

- Headlines on magazine covers aren't always tappable, even though we've known that users want this since our first iPad studies in early 2010. Honorable exceptions, including *Vanity Fair,* the *New Yorker,* and the other magazines that essentially copied their iPad versions, did allow users to tap a headline on the cover to go directly to the corresponding story (Figure 5.34).

- *Page view* is unreadable, and *Text view* has the worst layout we've seen in years. Illustrations are either too big or too small and are usually located far from the place they're discussed in the copy.

- The page scrubber is a singularly useless navigation device: It offers no overview of the available content and requires pixel-perfect finger movements. Even though this widget didn't help users at all in testing, several users said that they liked it, which is a great example of why you shouldn't listen to what users *say*. (Rather, you should watch what they *do*.) People felt so lost within the magazines that *any* navigation aid seemed to offer a lifeline, even when it was no good. Users aren't designers, so they don't know that there are many other navigation features that could have been chosen instead.

- The pop-up table of contents often contained "cute" headlines that might work in print but emitted zero information scent. Article summaries were no better.

- Search was like watching AltaVista redux. Actually, AltaVista was better in late 1998 than magazine/newspaper search on the Kindle Fire today, because at least AltaVista *tried* to prioritize the search results instead of simply listing all keyword matches.

Screen updates are too slow, so scrolling can feel erratic and there's a huge lag in response after pressing command buttons. This breaks the illusion of direct manipulation.

Using apps and websites on the Kindle Fire is less efficient than on other devices because it lacks two key physical buttons: one to return to the home screen (as on the Kindle Keyboard) and one for volume up/down (as on the iPad). A physical Back button would also make the interaction more fluent (as on Android phones). For those apps that dim the virtual buttons to reclaim more screen space, users have to touch the screen to bring up the control strip containing those buttons. After a while this interaction becomes less unnatural, but it's still an extra step compared to tapping a hard button. As for the full keyboard, though, good riddance. It's a waste to allocate room for all the A–Z keys on a small device, and most use doesn't require more typing than you can comfortably achieve with an onscreen keyboard.

The Kindle Fire also suffers from plain, old, bad UI design in many areas. For example, the highlighting feedback for touching a button is so small that your finger usually covers it, making it invisible, as shown in **Figure 5.35**.

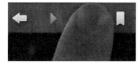

Figure 5.35 Look closely and you can see the corner of the highlighting around the button being pushed, but the user's finger often covers such feedback completely.

Making feedback big enough to be seen around the user's finger is a basic usability guideline for visual design for mobile and tablets—a big mistake by Amazon. Another example of bad design that tripped up several users in our testing is that the Silk Web browser lets users select individual words within the text in drop-down menus. In fact, it's so easy to do this that users often selected words when they wanted to activate a menu option.

If we were given to conspiracy theories, we'd say that Amazon deliberately designed a poor Web browsing user experience to keep Fire users from shopping on competing sites. Amazon's own built-in shopping app has great usability, so it clearly knows how to design for the tablet.

Seven-inch tablet UX prospects: great or terrible?

Seven-inch tablets have either a glorious future or will fail miserably. We doubt there's a middle path in their future.

For 7-inch tablets to succeed, service and content providers must design specifically for these devices. Repurposed designs from print, mobile phones, 10-inch tablets, or desktop PCs will fail, because they offer a terrible user experience. A 7-inch tablet is a sufficiently different form factor that must be treated as a new platform. In addition, these mid-sized tablets are so weak that suboptimal designs—that is, repurposed content—won't work. Optimize for 7-inch or die.

Pragmatically it won't pay for magazine publishers, websites, application programmers, and other providers to design and build a separate version of their offerings for 7-inch tablets unless these devices have many millions of users. Unless there's a substantial payoff, the expense of maintaining multiple versions will be too great.

That's why our prediction for the 7-inch future is bimodal. *If* the platform becomes a raving success and quickly sells in large numbers (say, 50 million copies by the end of 2013), *then* we'll have an economic foundation to support a rich ecosystem of 7-inch-optimized services. And, with plentiful offerings, users will be satisfied and will buy more 7-inch devices—a virtuous circle.

On the other hand, *if* only a few million 7-inch tablets sell over the next year or two, *then* the platform will either die or be reduced to serving those people who can't afford a full-sized tablet. A small audience won't offer much incentive for providers to publish 7-inch-optimized content and services. The resulting unpleasant user experience will drive any remaining affluent users to buy bigger tablets—a vicious circle.

Seven-inch tablets occupy a tenuous slice of territory in the user experience landscape:

- On the one hand, the devices are too weak to support easy, pleasant, and efficient use of the broad range of user interfaces optimized for other form factors. Seven-inch screens are too small to easily browse full websites and yet too big to carry with you at all times like a mobile phone.

- On the other hand, they are strong enough to provide good usability when designs are optimized for the 7-inch platform. The screen is large enough to show pretty pictures and full-color illustrations, and it can also support fairly efficient navigation and other user actions. When designed right, the 7-inch user experience is richer and more pleasant than a mobile phone UX.

Designs that are optimized for 7-inch tablets will have high usability. They'll probably never fully equal a 10-inch UX, but then again, the 7-inch devices are much cheaper and easier to carry around. Hopefully future 7-inch tablets will also be lighter and have longer battery life than the current bulkier devices.

Will the economics support the availability of such optimized designs? We don't know, because user research and usability analysis can't take us into that territory. All we can say is that the UX will be great if the money is there and poor if it's not. For now, 7-inch tablets will have to make do with repurposed content.

6 Looking Toward the Future

The title of this book is *Mobile Usability*, but in truth we've covered only telephones and tablets. Even worse, because we hardly discussed feature phones, almost everything in the book so far has been about flat touch screens—from small touch screens on phones to big touch screens on tablets. In this chapter we take a broader view of mobile computing and consider other types of user interfaces we may see in the future.

Three big trends have occurred in the history of computing: computers have been getting smaller, cheaper, and used in more and more contexts—from mainframes to PCs to mobile—and beyond. We expect the future to bring even smaller computers that will cost a pittance and be used for many things that we don't know how to compute today.

We expect one more major development that hasn't been prominent in the history of computing—more diversity of devices. In the past there was usually one type of computer that was dominant:

- In the mainframe era, Big Blue (IBM) was everywhere and the "seven dwarves" (IBM's smaller competitors) shipped computers that looked pretty much the same.

- In the PC era, Microsoft Windows was everywhere and the only real competitor (Macintosh) looked pretty much the same—at least after 1995.

- Currently almost all smartphones look the same, and tablets look like oversized smartphones.

We think that each user will be using many computers in the future and that many of these devices will be quite different from each other. Why? First, this is a function of computers becoming dirt cheap. Why limit yourself to one? Second, as computers fill ever-more ecological niches, they'll do their job better if they are optimized for various specialized circumstances.

Transmedia Design for the Three Screens

Many people predict that mobile devices will be the only important user interface (UI) platform in the so-called "post-PC" future. Some even recommend designing websites for mobile first and then modifying the design for the desktop PC as an afterthought.

We disagree.

Although it makes for a good story to claim that something new will kill the old, things rarely work out that way. As Peter Zollman once said, "With the possible exception of the town crier, a new medium has never put an old medium out of business." Despite TV, we still have radio—and, for that matter, live theater. In the computer industry, we still have mainframes, and IBM harvests billions each year accordingly.

Computers are already so cheap that most people in rich countries own several devices: one for each major need. Of course, under the moniker "computer" we include not just PCs, but also tablets, phones, mainframes, and servers. Sure, most homes won't have a mainframe in the basement, but many have a family file server to host their photo and video libraries.

PCs Will Remain Important

Desktop PCs have two inherent advantages over mobile:

- Much larger screens, letting users see more information at a glance. This enhances content comprehension, facilitates navigation and interleaved browsing, and supports compare-and-contrast tasks, which are often the most critical high-value tasks.

- Better input devices, with a big keyboard and a real mouse.

Big screens and big input devices are both inherent advantages of the desktop PCs; mobile devices must be small so users can carry them around. Desktop PCs have additional advantages that will hold for at least the next decade: faster bandwidth; hardware oomph, such as faster processors, more memory, and larger hard drives; software maturity; and printing.

Bandwidth and hardware–software prowess are only temporary advantages for desktop PCs. Because mobile moves at a faster pace, it will eventually reach a level sufficient to support most user needs in these areas.

However, better input and better output are durable advantages for the desktop user experience (UX).

We are screen-size bigots: Bigger screens deliver hugely higher user productivity. Anyone who's experienced a 30-inch monitor cringes at the idea of doing a major project on anything smaller. It's astounding that PC makers don't offer even bigger screens.

Much use will shift from desktops to phones and tablets, but a big percentage of use will remain on the desktop. It's difficult to estimate the exact percentage for each device class, but it's fairly certain that much high-value use will stay predominantly on desktop. Thus the percentage split of value between devices will be more favorable to the PC, even as the percentage split of time turns increasingly more toward tablets and phones.

The Third Screen: TV

After mobile devices and desktop PCs, the third main category of screen-based UX is television. It's quite valuable, ranging from 20 cents to $2 per hour of user time. (Jakob pays the cable company about $2/viewer hour, but his household watches much less TV than most families. Amazon.com charges $1.99 to stream any *Star Trek* episode, which also seems on the high end.)

We focus on mobile and desktop usability because so few companies engage in TV-based interaction design. Usability is typically horrible, and with the advent of DVR mobile apps created by cable companies, more and more users rely on their phones and tablets to program their DVR or even to change channels. However, there's some hope for the future, as exemplified by the Kinect gestural UI.

Currently, designing for TV is relevant primarily for companies in the entertainment or consumer electronics industries. If interactive TV usability improves substantially, more companies will need to pay attention to this platform. At that point, one fact is certain: TV will need a third UI that's distinct from your mobile and desktop designs.

Transmedia User Experience

Most companies will probably deploy only two UI designs: mobile and desktop. Others might need more, depending on their industry. Whatever the number, there are two key points to remember:

- Create separate and distinct UI designs for device categories that are sufficiently different.

- Retain the feel of a product family across devices, despite the different UIs and different feature sets. This requires a transmedia design strategy.

Screens 4 and 5: Tiny, Huge

As if it weren't enough to design two or three different UIs for mobile, desktop, and possibly TV, there are two even more extreme screen sizes to consider: very, very small and very, very large. Again, each will need its own UI.

Tiny screens include the postage-sized displays on lots of consumer electronics—even a toothbrush has its own display these days. If we stretch the definition a bit, we can also include the user experiences driven by items with embedded RFID chips and QR codes.

Huge screens range from meeting-room–sized displays to smart buildings, and even smart campuses, such as hospitals, that guide visitors and patients to the right buildings and rooms.

As yet there hasn't been much usability work done on these two extremes, but they definitely have their own challenges. And for sure, any decent UI will have to be very different from those on phones and desktop PCs.

Our experience with transmedia usability is not yet sufficient to provide an exhaustive list of guidelines for achieving a cohesive UX across platforms. But we know that it's essential to get the following four issues right:

- **Visual continuity.** Obviously UIs will look different on different screen sizes, but they should look similar enough to feel like they were cut from the same cloth. No, it's not enough to have the same logo or the same color scheme. The interactive elements also must have a similar look. Layouts will clearly differ, but users should still feel confident about where to locate information as they move between platforms.

- **Feature continuity.** The smaller the device, the smaller the feature set you can comfortably provide. However, users should still feel that the same main features are available in all locations. Even more important, they should feel that the features work consistently, even if they've been simplified. Let's say, for example, that your e-commerce site offers product ratings. Your mobile site and your full site should use the same rating scale, but maybe your mobile site doesn't let users enter new reviews or doesn't show the full text of existing reviews by default. Designed correctly, however, users will still feel that they get the benefit of the full site's reviews while using the mobile site.

- **Data continuity.** The user's data should be the same in all locations. Because of different feature sets, some data might not be available everywhere, but anything accessible in multiple places should be the same. Users shouldn't have to "sync" as a separate action.

- **Content continuity.** We know that you must write much more concisely for mobile than for desktop use. But the basic content strategy should be the same; in particular, you should use a similar *tone of voice* for all platforms, so that you "sound" the same everywhere. For example, children love characters in Web design. If you use them, your mobile site might not have room for all the creatures but should include the lead characters from the full site. (This will also promote visual continuity: The characters should look basically the same, even when drawn with fewer pixels. For that matter, character reuse also promotes feature continuity to the extent that navigation is based around the characters.)

To conclude, cross-platform UIs should be *different* but *similar*.

Beyond Flatland

Desktop computers, mobile phones, and televisions still have flat screens. We need to get more aggressively diverse in our future thinking.

Computers will have all shapes and forms, although most of these may not be immediately recognizable as a computer. Our colleague in Nielsen Norman Group, Don Norman, called this "the invisible computer" in his book with that title, *The Invisible Computer*, (The MIT Press, 1999). The computer as such disappears, and the world becomes computational.

There are several ways of building a computational environment. The most radical is to abandon the real world and inhabit an artificial one. Virtual reality (VR) is often achieved by wearing a helmet or all-enclosing goggles, so that the user sees only images projected by the computer. When everything you see is a computer image, it's as if you're living inside the computer.

Less-immersive VR interfaces can be built by projecting images on all the walls, the ceiling, and the floor of a special room. Think of the *Star Trek* holodeck, although usually without deficient safety protocols, because most VR systems are purely visual and can't shoot you.

VR probably has a great future for games and for certain specialized tasks, such as remote-controlled surgery. But for most everyday and business tasks, we are not big VR fans, because it seems too big a sacrifice to give up the real world. Living inside a helmet is not for most people.

Augmented reality (AR) is more promising. Here, we stay in the real world but overlay it with a slight coating of data. Google Glasses are the most popular current AR system, but researchers have worked on such designs for decades. The most classic example is being at a cocktail party and seeing the name of every guest projected next to their face. A good system would also summarize your past interactions with that guest and remind you of any pending issues you wanted to bring up.

Figure 6.1 shows an idea we had in 2001 for a data overlay on airplane windows. Passengers can look out the window and see general landmarks (Birch Lake) and locations of personal interest (Uncle Bob's house). The airlines can "rent" access to this feature much like they rent headphones for watching in-flight movies. Airlines might also sell advertising—for instance, to NFL to show locations of stadiums, or for chain amusement parks, restaurants, and so on.

Figure 6.1 Concept sketch from Nielsen Norman Group's 2001 visioneering project. An airplane passenger can call up an overlay map when looking out the window.

Projected repair manuals are another good AR example. As the mechanic crawls around inside an airplane engine, simply looking at a component will display readouts of its critical data together with historical information about its past performance and predictions of time-to-failure. If the mechanic wanted to know more about a specific component, a blink of the eye or a spoken command will bring up schematics and other information that would otherwise be available only by crawling back out of the engine and flipping through a handbook. Even having the same information on a touch tablet would not be nearly as convenient as seeing it displayed right over each component. For one thing, the engine becomes the UI, and it's certainly also better to have hands-free operation when you're trying to repair something.

We just painted an idyllic picture of well functioning AR systems. But all user interfaces raise usability issues, and AR is no exception. Data overload is certainly one looming usability problem, and the design will also have to manage distractions.

The more we mess with reality, the more we also raise ethical questions. Think of the ability to "skin" the video image of yourself, as projected through future versions of technologies like Skype and FaceTime. Simple AR modifications to the outgoing video could make you appear to wear a nicer suit and be in a busy office environment instead of hanging out at the beach. **Figure 6.2** shows an idea for creating an "Association for Truth in Skins" (ATIS) to certify the realism of a user's projected image.

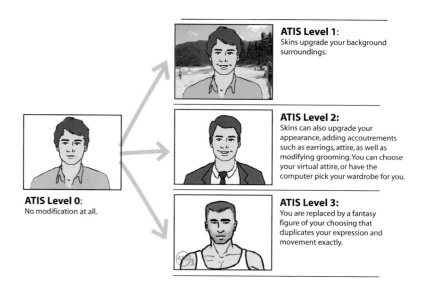

ATIS Level 1:
Skins upgrade your background surroundings.

ATIS Level 2:
Skins can also upgrade your appearance, adding accoutrements such as earrings, attire, as well as modifying grooming. You can choose your virtual attire, or have the computer pick your wardrobe for you.

ATIS Level 3:
You are replaced by a fantasy figure of your choosing that duplicates your expression and movement exactly.

ATIS Level 0:
No modification at all.

Your own body can also become part of the computer. Actual brain-wave scanning is fairly far into the future, except for extreme cases like controlling prosthetic limbs. But Microsoft's Kinect system already observes the user through cameras and reacts to movements and gestures that are made without touching anything. With an application such as Your Shape: Fitness Evolved (**Figure 6.3**), the user simply works out in front of the camera, and the computer provides real-time feedback on exercise form ("do deeper squats") while representing the user as a silhouette on the screen.

Figure 6.3 Screen shot from the Kinect application Your Shape: Fitness Evolved. Commands are issued by gestures: here by having the user reach for an empty point in space that corresponds to making the onscreen silhouette touch a button.

In the Future, We'll All Be Harry Potter

By saying that one day we'll be like Harry Potter, we don't mean that people will fly around on broomsticks or play three-dimensional ballgames (although virtual reality will let enthusiasts play Quidditch matches). What we do mean is that we're about to experience a world where spirit inhabits formerly inanimate objects.

Much of the Harry Potter books' charm comes from the quirky magic objects that surround Harry and his friends. Rather than being solid and static, these objects embody initiative and activity. This is precisely the shift we'll experience as computational power moves beyond the desktop into everyday objects.

Next-generation Magic

Here are some examples of agency in Harry Potter's objects, and how we'll achieve similar powers in the future:

- The *Daily Prophet* newspaper has photos that come alive when the wizards look at them. Tablets already allow us to read multimedia news at the breakfast table. Combined with eyetracking (which is still a few releases away), we'll rid ourselves of those annoying, constantly moving video clips. Instead, videos will appear as still images that play only when you indicate interest by looking at them for half a second or more.

- Socks scream loudly when they become too smelly. Developers could implement this feature using sensors, either in the socks (wearable computing) or in the environment. Smart clothing is one of the main research directions for the future of computing.

- Action figures move around, exhibiting the personality of famous Quidditch players. Ever since Interactive Barney, we've had toys with some amount of autonomy. Personality, however, is still missing.

- The Pensieve stores thoughts and memories for later retrieval. Digital cameras will capture ever-bigger parts of our experience, especially as they're integrated with mobile devices that know our agenda and the people we're meeting with. Perhaps we'll even be able to subscribe to the videos of ourselves taken by the ever-present security surveillance cameras.

- Mirrors comment on the reflectee's appearance. This will surely be a commercial product. In the far future, expert systems might issue the commentary, but in the interim it could be provided by networked fashion consultants: either cheap staff in low-salary countries or busybodies who will gladly appraise other people for free.

- Omniculars offer instant replay. We already have binoculars with built-in digital cameras. Combined with the instant replay technology offered by systems like TiVo, you have first-generation omniculars. Add-ons could include an expert system for bird-spotting that would match any bird with an ornithological database and annotate the image with the bird's common and Latin names.

- The Marauder's Map has icons that represent people as they move around Hogwarts Castle. Smart badges already let us track employee movement in high-security facilities. Your trusty cellphone brings the same feature to open spaces, pending only privacy concerns.

We are not so nerdy as to suggest that you read Harry Potter as an idea manual for next-generation product development. But the books are filled with examples of products that we'll soon be able to build, and they do provide some idea of what it might mean to embody awareness in the physical world.

Don't Harm the Muggles

Harry Potter's world resembles the world of computers in another way as well: In the Harry Potter books, the population consists of two distinct groups—a small group of wizards and a much larger group of Muggles (standard-issue humans) who know nothing about magic or the dealings of wizards.

Similarly, in our world, the vast majority of people don't understand computers or technology. Science fiction author Arthur C. Clarke once said that "Any sufficiently advanced technology is indistinguishable from magic." Unfortunately computers and the Internet are this "advanced technology" as far as most people are concerned. Things appear on their screens, computers deliver the desired results, and how it happens is all just so much magic.

In the Harry Potter books, the ethical wizards have agreed to leave the Muggles alone and not do magic tricks on them. It seems that computer wizards have something to learn from Harry Potter, because they often use their power in ways that are harmful to regular people.

We typically argue against poor Internet usability because it reduces a company's ability to generate business value from its website. Bad customer service equals fewer customers. However, the bigger picture is even worse: Every screen that doesn't conform to expected behavior and design conventions undermines users' ability to build a conceptual model of the Web, and thus reduces their ability to use other sites with ease, confidence, and pleasure. Designers who inflict poor usability on the world and its Muggles are wicked wizards indeed.

A Bit of History

This appendix contains a short
description of our first mobile usability
study, which we ran way back in 2000.
At the time, we tested people using
WAP (Wireless Application Protocol)
phones to access the online services
of the day.

WAP was an early way of accessing
the Internet through mobile phones.
However, after we saw the usability
findings, we started saying that the
acronym WAP really stands for Wrong
Approach to Portability.

The full 99-page report from our WAP study is available as a free download from our website at www.nngroup.com/reports/wap. The detailed analyses of specific WAP screens are irrelevant these days unless you're one of the unfortunate people who still have to design for feature phones. But many of the general patterns of user behaviors are still important.

We tell you about this early research for three reasons:

- It's always satisfying to gloat, so it's good to see how far the use of mobile devices has come since these first days of mobile Internet use.

- It's interesting to note how several of the early findings match the results of current user research. Despite revolutionary changes in the technology, people still want to do many of the same tasks on their mobile devices. For example, we found that killing time is a killer app for mobile in 2000, and that's still true.

- Industry reactions to our research serve as a cautionary tale. The telephony industry issued a press release denouncing us for having tested too few users for too short a time to draw valid conclusions.

As to the last point, we're very used to having partisan groups reject our usability findings. This happens every time we recommend something other than whatever technology or designs somebody is profiting from promoting. We, of course, have no agenda other than reporting how average users actually behave, so it's of no consequence to us if powerful companies try to make money from suppressing human needs.

In the case of our WAP study, it's true that we tested too few users to draw strong statistical findings. So when we found that 70 percent of the test participants rejected the technology, the true number from a bigger study might easily have been 60 percent or 80 percent. However, that doesn't matter. It was clear that a) most people didn't like WAP, and b) all users had severe problems getting anything done with these user interfaces.

In addition, although it might not seem like a week is a long time to use WAP phones, the unfortunate truth is that any consumer technology that people can't use after a week is doomed.

With the benefit of hindsight, we can now say that history has forcefully vindicated us. Mobile information access never took off until much better user interfaces were introduced with the iPhone in 2007. WAP was relegated to the dustbin of history—no matter how viciously its advocates tried to repudiate our usability findings.

You can't fight billions of users. Having the people on our side is why we tend to win in the end.

The rest of this appendix was written in 2000. The text has been lightly edited for inclusion in this book, but all the conclusions were drawn at the time. We haven't rewritten history to benefit from our current level of knowledge about mobile usability.

Figure A.1 The Ericsson R320s was one of the WAP phones in our study.

Field Study in 2000

In the fall of 2000, we ran a field study of WAP users in London. After a week's experience using WAP, study participants had one resounding conclusion: 70 percent of them said they would not be using WAP in a year.

For the study, we gave 20 users a WAP phone, asked them to use it for a week, and asked them to record their impressions in a diary. We also performed traditional usability tests with users at the beginning and end of the week. We gave half of the users an Ericsson R320s (**Figure A.1**) and the other half a Nokia 7110e.

Figure A.1 shows a picture of the Ericsson R320s. The five-line screen shows a typical homepage from a WAP portal with links to various topics. Below the screen are navigation buttons to move the cursor. There's also a scroll wheel on the side of the phone, just below the antenna. The Yes button confirms the selection, and the No button works as a Back function. Believe it or not, this was considered a very high-end phone in 2000.

We ran this study in London because of the advanced state of the United Kingdom's mobile phone market relative to the United States. The UK's WAP services had been under development longer than those in the United States and were also more widely deployed at the time of our study.

It is important to note that users provided their negative review of WAP after a full week of hands-on experience with the technology. It is irrelevant to ask people in a focus group to predict whether they would like something they have not tried, so the only way to get valid data is to let users experience the technology before you ask them for their opinions.

WAP Doesn't Work

Of course, we didn't just collect opinions. We ran timed task-performance studies as well, because observations are the best source of data. We asked users to accomplish simple tasks with their WAP phones at the beginning of the week and at the end. **Table A.1** shows some of our findings.

In Table A.1, the first number indicates the mean number of minutes users needed to perform the task in the beginning of our study, and the second number indicates the mean measurement at the end of the study.

Table A.1 Time to Perform Typical Tasks with WAP Phones

Task	Start of Study	After a Week
Read world headlines	1.3 min.	1.1 min.
Check local weather forecast	2.7 min.	1.9 min.
Read TV program listing	2.6 min.	1.6 min.

As the table shows, our basic conclusion is that WAP usability failed miserably; accomplishing even the simplest of tasks took much too long to provide any user satisfaction. It simply should not take two minutes to find the current weather forecast or what will be showing on BBC1 at 8 p.m.

We asked a group of Internet experts how long they thought these tasks should take (before showing them our data), and most estimated a task time of less than 30 seconds. Considering that, at the time, WAP users paid for airtime by the minute, one of our users calculated that it would have been cheaper for her to buy a newspaper and throw away everything but the TV listings than to look up that evening's BBC programs on her WAP phone.

Déjà Vu: 1994 All Over Again

Our findings from this WAP usability study in late 2000 bear a striking resemblance to several Web usability studies we conducted in 1994 (the age of Mosaic). It was truly déjà vu: Many of our conclusions were the same as those we reached at the dawn of the Web. Hopefully the evolution of mobile use will follow that of the Web: When websites got better in subsequent years (especially around 1997), many more users started accessing the Web, and commercial use exploded.

The usability of current WAP services is severely reduced because of a misguided use of design principles from traditional Web design. This situation is exactly equivalent to Web design problems in 1994, when many sites contained "brochureware" that followed design principles that worked great in print (say, big images) but didn't work in an interactive medium.

For example, we came across a WAP design from Excite that used four screens to present two screens' worth of material (**Figure A.2**). The design even had a splash screen. To add insult to injury, the fourth screen that purportedly contained the actual article (Figure A.2D) didn't add any new information to that contained in the headline,

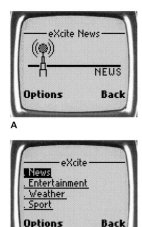

A

B

C

D

Figure A.2 Users had to navigate four screens to see a miserly two lines of news about the Hatfield railroad line: (**A**) splash screen; (**B**) menu of news categories; (**C**) menu of headlines; (**D**) article page.

as shown on the previous screen. A clear design guideline for presenting information on small screens is to avoid repeating content that the user has just seen. We discovered this in 2000, and it's still true. (Splash screens, of course, are a poor design choice in any year.)

Such lavish design may work on the Web if users have a big-screen PC, but on a small-screen device, designers must boil down each service to its essence and show much less information.

Our users often faced unclear labels and menu choices written in special language invented by the WAP designer. NewSpeak was rampant in the Web's infancy, and many sites invented cute vocabulary for their services in a misguided attempt to brand their site with proprietary language. This didn't work. Users want a no-brainer design that uses standard terms for standard features. The need for simple language is even stronger in WAP design, because there is no room to explain nonstandard terminology with roll-over effects, icons, or captions.

Several WAP services that we tested were unnecessarily difficult to use because of a mismatch between their information architecture and the users' tasks. For example, TV listings were organized by television network, meaning that you would have to go to several different parts of the service to find out what was on at 8 p.m. (one screen for BBC1, another screen for BBC2, and so on in an annoyingly slow sequence of screens).

Very precise task analysis would have been necessary for WAP services to succeed. Unfortunately task analysis is a black art as far as most people are concerned, and it is the least appreciated part of usability engineering. The traditional Web also suffers from poor task analysis: Many sites are structured according to how company management thinks rather than how users typically approach their tasks. Although poor task support is a serious usability problem for a big-screen website, it is a usability catastrophe for a small-screen WAP service. With the big screen, users can see many more alternative options; thus, it is not so critical that designers pick exactly the right ones at each step. For WAP, be right or be dead.

One WAP usability finding that we have not seen on the Web was a lack of clear differentiation between services. As one of our users noted when comparing the *Financial Times* and *The Guardian*, in the real world you'll have trouble finding two more different newspapers. On WAP, however, you can't tell them apart.

Websites usually suffer from the opposite problem: They are much too different. With WAP, the service's expressive power is severely reduced because of the need to squeeze everything into extremely short menus and present all content in ultra-short condensed versions. Service providers must cultivate a new appreciation for language and hire copywriters who can develop a distinct voice in a minimum word count. This will be the real way to distinguish WAP services.

Mobile Killer App: Killing Time

Promising mobile Internet services follow a bi modal distribution with two dramatically contrasting approaches that both work well with users:

- Highly goal-driven services aimed at providing fast answers to specific problems. Examples include: "My flight was canceled; get me a new airline reservation" and "What's the weather?"

- Entertainment-focused services whose sole purpose is killing time. Examples include gossip, games, and sports services. Gossip is particularly suited for WAP because the content can be very brief and still be satisfying.

Mobile services must target users with immediate, context-directed content. General services like shopping are less likely to succeed in the mobile environment. Indeed, in the list of services bookmarked by users, shopping hardly figures at all; sports and entertainment are the two big categories.

Killing time is a perfect application for mobile devices because they are readily available when users are waiting around for something to happen. At the bus stop? Play a short game. In line for something? Read a paragraph of gossip. Stuck in traffic that doesn't move? Check the scores of your favorite teams.

Index

M

Macy's mobile app, 125
magazine apps
    iPad, 146–147, 149–150,
      156–157, 158, 161
    Kindle Fire, 174–177
Mail app for iPad, 163–164
Martha Stewart Cocktails app,
   139, 154
Marvel Comics app, 84, 155
mega menus, 163
memorability of gestures,
   141–143
Microsoft Kinect system, 188
Microsoft Surface tablets, 166
mini-information architecture
   (mini-IA), 123–129
    alphabetical sorting used in,
      124–126
    linear paging used in, 123–124
    usage-driven structure and,
      129
    usage-relevant structure and,
      127–129
mobile apps, 41–44
    chrome used in, 57
    registration issues, 81–86
    WSJ case study, 86–99
mobile device classes, 15–18
    explanation of, 15–16
    separate designs for, 17–18
mobile intranets, 47
mobile usability studies. *See*
  usability studies
mobile websites
    apps vs., 34–41
    arguments against, 21–22
    design ideas for, 20–21
    download times for, 79–81
    filling in forms on, 77–78
    full websites vs., 18–33
    guidelines for building, 18–20
    iPad display of, 133
    screen optimization, 67–76
    typing on, 76–79
    usability issues, 50–51
    user testing of, 75–76
    wasted space on, 52–67
Monetate study, viii–ix
Moore's Law, 35
mouse vs. finger input, 24–25

N

NASA's iPad app, 162–163
National Geographic website, 19
native apps, 40
navigation bars, 13, 72
navigation problems, 159–165
NBC.com website, 11, 123
Net-a-porter app, 78, 121, 122
New York Times
    iPad apps, 140–141, 151
    mobile apps, 71
New Yorker magazine app, 146–147
newspapers
    mobile apps, 71, 79, 121,
      147–149, 151
    survival imperatives, 91
    WSJ app case study, 86–99
Nielsen, Jakob, 6, 88, 165, 171
Nielsen Company, 14
Nielsen Norman Group, 2, 14, 186
Nielsen's Law, 35
90-9-1 rule, 88
noises, startup, 165–166
Nordstrom mobile site, 96, 97
Norman, Don, 141, 186
Notability app, 143, 144
NPR mobile site, 70

O

OpenAppMkt Web app, 39
open-ended tasks, 5
Orchestra app, 82, 83, 93
orientation views, 166–167
OSHA Heat Safety Tool app, 107
overloaded commands, 63–66

P

Palo Alto Research Center, 73
PayPal, using for purchases, 12
perceived affordances, 141
physical vs. virtual buttons, 37
physical vs. virtual keyboards,
   76–77
pinch-zoom gesture, 63
Pirolli, Peter, 73
Pizza Hut app, 84–86, 87
Playboy Web app, 38
popovers, 164–165
Popular Science app, 149–150,
   151–152, 175
portrait orientation, 166–167

print metaphor, 151–153
Prioritizing Web Usability (Nielsen
   & Loranger), 6
privacy policies, 102
progressive disclosure, 59, 60,
   118–119
ProPublica website, 31–32, 114,
   115
publication date info, 71

Q

qualitative user research, 5–7
QVC iPad app, 136

R

Raskin, Jef, 153
reading comprehension, 102–108
    Cloze test of, 103–104
    mobile devices and, 102,
      104–108
Recalls.gov app, 107, 108
recognition-based user interfaces,
   142
registration requirement
    Pizza Hut example, 84–86, 87
    problems with, 81–84
research. *See* usability studies
responsive design, 28–33
Rue La La app, 136

S

scannability, 69
screen shots, x–xi
screens
    extremes of tiny and huge, 184
    limitations of small, 50–51, 52
    optimizing for mobile use,
      67–76
    transmedia design for, 182–185
    wasted space on, 52–55
    See also user interfaces
scroll vs. card model, 153
scrolling
    designing into iPad apps,
      156–157
    mobile device problems with,
      10, 11
search engine optimization
   (SEO), 111
search engine results page
   (SERP), 111

W

Wall Street Journal
- mobile app case study, 86–99
- mobile website layering, 120–121

Walmart mobile site, 96, 97

WAP (wireless access protocol), 17
- mobile usability study, 44, 193–198
- modern phone comparison study, 44–45

Washington Post app, 114, 115

wasted mobile space, 52–55

Weather Bug app, 55

Weather Channel app, 52, 53, 155

Web apps, 38–39, 40, 42

Web browser chrome, 57

Web usability studies, 196

WebMD mobile app, 121, 122

websites
- chrome on, 57
- full vs. mobile, 18–33
- homepage for, 64
- iPad display of, 133
- links to/from, 19–20
- usability guidelines, 82
- *See also* mobile websites

Wikipedia mobile site, 20, 118–119

Windows OS chrome, 56

Wolfram Alpha app, 83

workflow design
- importance of, 96–97
- *WSJ* case example, 94–95, 98–99

writing for mobile, 101–129
- author biographies and, 114
- byline pros and cons in, 112–115
- deferring information in, 116–122
- eliminating filler in, 109–111
- examples of good and bad, 106–108
- importance of conciseness in, 25–26, 33
- layering information in, 120–122
- old, familiar words used in, 111–112
- reading comprehension and, 102–108
- secondary screens used in, 116–122
- structuring content in, 123–129

WSJ mobile app case study, 86–99
- brand degradation issues, 90–91
- business model consideration, 95
- screen design improvements, 91–94
- startup screen confusion, 89–90
- workflow redesign, 94–95, 98–99

Y

Yelp mobile site, 20, 54

You Are Your Own Gym app, 127–128

Z

Zapd app, 82, 96

Zappos
- Android app, 65, 79
- iPad app, 146, 147
- mobile website, 80, 81, 97

Zite app, 114, 115

Zollman, Peter, 182